P9-DEA-749

Dronings from a Queen Bee:
The First Five Years

To my parents, who brought me into being,
Tom, who led me to bee,
Jessica, Ben and Becca who give me reasons to be,
Marshall, who makes every day as sweet as honey and
Melvin, who won't let me be!
(If you find cat hair on your book, it is undoubtedly his.)

Table of Contents

My Beekeeping Life 1
  Angels with Real Wings 2
  Why Do I Keep Bees? 5
  A Bee in my Bonnet 7
  Why We Really Remodeled the House 11
  Halloween 13
  Bigfoot is a Beekeeper 15
  Cuddled to Death 18
  My Favorite Things About Bees 22
  Pictorial of the Honey Process 25
  My Drone 27

This Keeping of Bees 33
  We May Bee Prone to Exaggeration 34
  Go Blue 36
  30,000 Tiny Winter Coats 38
  The Importance of a Bee Veil and Chocolate 40
  Beekeeper Fantasies 43
  Yes, Bees Die 44
  How Can an Insect so Small Require So Much Storage Space? 47
  Really? 50

Swarming 55
  Pants Are Overrated 57
  Up, Up and Away 60
  Swarming to the Party 63
  Why Do Bees Swarm? 66
  Splitting to Prevent Swarming 69
  Just Split, Before They Split 71
  Stars, Stripes and Bees 73
  Bee Careful What You Wish For 76
  Photo Story of a Swarming Event 80
  Swarming Summary 81

Bee-ing in Their Presence 83
  Thunder? I Won't Use the Metal Stepladder 84
  Where Some of the Hours Go 87
  Bee Disease Flare-Up 88
  Dad's Bees 90
  Beeks, Bearding and Other Oddities 94
  Queen Bee to Be 96

In Summary 99

My Beekeeping Life

The first time I pulled on a protective bee veil I
thought, "This is SO not right." You have to think twice
if what you're doing for fun and relaxation
requires protective equipment.

As you'll soon read though, I didn't have the luxury of thinking twice about
keeping bees.

While I don't wish the circumstances that led me to beekeeping on anyone,
they were a silver lining in a very dark cloud. If I hadn't started beekeeping, I
would've missed out on one of the best things in my life.

Just last summer, I spent most of a glorious day checking hives, safely seeing
everything through the screen of my protective veil. Putting on the protective bee
suit had initially felt foreboding and ominous, but now I'm very comfortable with it.

Perhaps too comfortable...

That evening I walked outside through a sliding screen door, and by "through,"
well, I mean through. Sure, I saw the screen in front of my face. My brain
registered it as the bee veil's screen, not the one attached to the house.

I picked myself up off the ground, awkwardly climbing out of what was left
of the bent door frame and torn screen. The bees in the backyard erupted in
laughter. With nothing injured except my pride, there was nothing to do but
join them.

I strive to find the lighter side of most things, although I'll warn you, you
wouldn't think that by reading the first essay of this collection. Some people
have told me they found it quite depressing.

If it hits you hard, I apologize, but please keep reading. It is an important part
of my first five years of beekeeping. It sadly describes the end of one love story,
but also launches a second one, my love affair with an insect.

Even an insect that too often laughs at me.

Angels with Real Wings

I'm a beekeeper because my husband Tom spent his life fearing all things medical. He never had regular check-ups. He ignored family history, extensive nagging, and significant signs that something was terribly wrong with his body. When he finally went to a doctor, he was diagnosed with very advanced stage IV colorectal cancer. Since

Tom's Bee-Loved Honey T-shirts were used to shroud the hives the evening he died.

it had remained undiagnosed for so long, it had evolved from a highly treatable disease to a likely fatal illness.

Tom gave it the good fight, surpassing all estimates on life expectancy and having about as much fun as you can have with terminal cancer, but he finally "flew" on a sunny day in late summer, with me and our children at his side.

Tommy left me with many things—including fantastic memories, unfinished home improvement projects, three awesome kids, and his beloved bees. Hundreds of thousands of them.

When life gives you lemons, you're supposed to make lemonade. When life gives you bees, they're supposed to make honey. Tom's bees are working on that; I'm trying to help.

... angels walk among us, wearing protective veils and carrying smokers.

During Tommy's battle with cancer, from February of 2008 until late August 2009, I met nurses and doctors who proved repeatedly that angels walk among us, wearing surgical scrubs and carrying charts.

Since then, I've met dozens of beekeepers who've proven repeatedly that angels walk among us, wearing

 © 2014 Charlotte Hubbard | www.hubbardhive.com

protective veils and carrying smokers. These beekeepers have helped me come to peace with "managing" the intriguing but sometimes overwhelming gift of bees, and they've also helped me come to peace with issues that can't be readily managed, like bees that don't want to stay in their hive... or grief.

When we were still in the throes of the battle, back in April of 2008, Tom had a second emergency surgery. Complications resulted, and during his month in the hospital, Hubby insisted I tend his bees until he could get home.

I said sure, I'd take care of his bees until he could again, but all of us (except Tom!) knew there was no point. The oncologist projected that Tom had only a few weeks to live, possibly a month or so at the most. She didn't want to tell him that quite yet though, not wanting to rob him of hope. She suggested we take him home to recover from surgery, and do whatever we could to make his final time on earth peaceful.

Thinking I'd be burying my husband before the summer of 2008 even started (and really needing him to tell me a few essential things, like how to mix lawn mower gas and where the safety deposit box key was), I wasn't happy about his spending his wee bit of energy instructing me on something I considered non-essential: assembling houses for bees. But instead of fading away like his doctors predicted, Tom instead began to shine. In his quest to fiddle with his bees, he gained weight instead of losing it, and climbed the stairs—a few more trips each day—to strengthen his shaky legs for visits to the hives at the bottom of our yard. I figured that the least I could do then was feign a little interest in his stinging insects, even if they were tremendously scary.

And buzzing loudly.

And increasing in numbers every day.

June 2008 passed. But Tommy, defying all medical predictions, did not.

And somewhere, in that blur of medical appointments, chemotherapy side effects, and the daily miracle of his survival, my keeping his bees became less of a chore and more of a blessing. When you're working with bees, it's best that you focus only on the bees and leave all worries elsewhere. If that focus wavers for a second, well, a sharp sting on the ankles is enough reminder about where priorities should "bee."

Tommy managed to continue to mock all medical predictions, and for another year we discussed bees, planned for them, and banged our heads against walls over them. Gradually I fell under this insect's magical spell. What were once "his" bees became "our" bees. Those bees were some of the sweetest times of our marriage.

Tommy gave cancer a good fight, but its defeat was not meant to "bee." We held his visitation in our backyard, amongst the gardens he so lovingly cultivated, outside of the garage whose contents would later take days for me to sort through (all the while wondering, "What was he thinking?!")

As the sun slipped over the horizon that blessed evening, hundreds of people gathered with us in our yard—hugging, crying, and laughing.

At the edge of our property, thousands of bees gathered in their hives. I don't know if they were laughing or crying, but I think they sensed things had changed. They respectfully gave us space, and vice versa. And, a few weeks later, they gave us pounds of glorious honey that we sold to raise money for Tom's favorite charities[1].

I never thought I'd be a beekeeper, but then, I never thought I'd be a widow before age 50 either. Both required going forward bravely, although, no matter how much smoke I might puff out of the smoker, or how many hours I spend behind the protective veil of my bee suit, I still can't fully hide from the grief that still knocks me down from time to time.

While I've gone forward bravely, I haven't gone forward alone. Beekeeping introduced me to a wonderful community of people for advice and support, and brought me the peace and companionship of a half-million buzzing friends.

There are angels among us, and sometimes they come in the form of perfect, fuzzy, golden insects.

Tom and Charlotte, with part of '09's honey crop.

1   See *www.tomsbelovedhoney.org*

Why Do I Keep Bees?

My son comes from a family of farmers, engineers, and other laborers, and he's dating a fabulous young woman from a very different social circle.

In our family, we read magazines. In hers, they're featured on the covers of them.

Her relatives are Ivy League professors, internationally known journalists, doctors or lawyers—except for those who are both doctors and lawyers.

I recently attended a gathering of "her people." They are kind, engaging and friendly. Because I can't eloquently discuss Mideast diplomacy, life-saving medical innovations (for which they hold the patents), or the merits of a Princeton versus a Yale PhD, I spent that intimidating evening hiding behind robust potted plants, except for occasional (OK, frequent) trips out to the awesome buffet for refills—especially from the dessert section.

In a classroom I'm in charge; in the apiary—
I'm perpetually the student. It seems that the longer
I keep bees, the stupider I get.

I'm introverted by nature, so I was quite comfortable hanging out with ferns. But somehow, word got out that I was a beekeeper. Elite, sophisticated people made a beeline to talk with me.

Like most beekeepers, I'm a bit shy and withdrawn. And like most beekeepers, that changes when it comes to talking about bees. People swarmed me with questions, and I moved from behind the sculpted bonsai, to beside it, to finally—in front of it. If I can't bee with my bees, I'll do the next best thing—talk about them.

As a beekeeper, I've spoken to several nursery and elementary schools, among other educational venues. From preschoolers to 4th graders, science camp kids to inner-city second graders, kids ask about the same dozen questions.

I found it amusing that PhDs and MDs ask about the same dozen questions as well! The highly intelligent and well-educated have so much in common with kindergartners. I make this observation not to mock anyone, but instead to

... whether you're following Wall Street or Sesame Street, honeybees are incredibly fascinating.

highlight what I think is one of the coolest things about honeybees: no matter whether you're following Wall Street or Sesame Street, honeybees are incredibly fascinating.

While the questions asked by kindergartners and patent lawyers were generally the same, I did give the older audience more complete information. For example, when asked "Have you ever been stung?" I told the kids "yes." I told the tax attorneys "yes, by both bees and bad investments."

To the question "Where do bees go in the winter?" I explained they generally stay snuggled in a group in the hive, but added for the adults "Except for those with the means to head south."

The doctors all nodded their heads in understanding. I'm sure most of them have the means to head south, to quite lovely "winter hives."

No matter the age and income level of the audience, I'm always asked, "Why do you keep bees?"

I share how we need pollinators, how local honey helps allergies and is a smart food, how I enjoy the perpetual learning and challenges of beekeeping. The gathering of investment bankers-attorneys-doctors then asked another question: "Is there a good ROI in keeping bees?"

I laughed at that question, a lot.

I have found that there's a *huge* ROI—a huge negative ROI if you just look at dollars and cents. If you look beyond the dollars to the fun of beekeeping, it pays huge dividends in working my mind, working my body, helping the planet and overall enjoyment.

The adults looked at me like they sort of understood, but I'm not sure they get it.

When I answer why I keep bees for kids, I give them the simple answer: Because bees are so cool.

The kids fully get it.

 © 2014 Charlotte Hubbard | www.hubbardhive.com

A Bee in My Bonnet

There are many sayings involving bees. Some of them are very understandable, like "making a beeline." If the meaning of that figure of speech eludes you, set out some chocolate ice cream and invite me over. I'll be happy to demonstrate.

You don't have to be a beekeeper for long to fully understand "busy as a bee." Honeybees are very industrious insects, and keeping them requires similar busyness at times.

If you do keep bees, you fully understand "like bees to honey." As soon as one of their gold-filled honeycombs is ruptured, they'll tend to it. If you ruptured it while working their hive and spilled a drop on your clothing, you'll quickly have lots of new friends cleaning it up for you. I understand that behavior. If there's a drop of honey on a biscuit I clean it up right away also.

It isn't obvious to me how the phrase "the bees' knees" evolved, but every time I see a bee up close, I try to see if she is bending any of her many legs. Or are those elbows?

Putting hives atop a barn roof seemed like a good idea at the time.

One of my favorite bee-related expressions is "bee in his (her) bonnet," a figure of speech I've used frequently. For years, I even thought I understood it. Thanks to recent events however, I now have a more thorough understanding.

I have the coordination of a newborn long-legged bird wearing a swim fin on one foot and a snow ski on the other. Upon imagining that, you're probably thinking "Wow, how do you get around?"

The short answer—with a lot of spilled cups of water, bruises, broken dishes and dramatic tumbles. Yes, I'm a klutz. Not a great characteristic for a beekeeper, as we often carry sharp hive tools and smokers.

Because I'm uncoordinated, and because I've worn my protective suit for several seasons now, it is a "Coat of Many Colors" with its pink duct tape here and blue duct tape there and silver stripes of duct tape to ensure there are no gaps or holes for bees to enter.

A *hive tool* is the beekeeper's best friend. It's an inexpensive but essential piece of perfectly shaped, sharp metal, and slightly larger than a bookmark.

It's used to pry open hives and pry apart frames with minimal damage.

It is also really handy for killing ticks.

Every time before I enter the hives, I'll spend a few moments examining myself in the mirror, to ensure there are no new holes or rips in the suit. When I tend the hives at my dad's farm, Dad will check me over for gaps. Dad takes this responsibility seriously each spring, but toward season's end, ironically when the bees are at their strongest, we both become a bit lax.

One September, before I opened the hives to add feeders, Dad gave my protective suit the once-over. He assured me that the veil was securely taped around the brim of my hat, and pronounced me invincible and ready to invade the home of hundreds of thousands of stinging insects. (Side note: professional sky divers check their own parachutes; they have a more vested interest. There's a lesson, one I should've realized.)

Dad's hives are atop his barn roof, a barn bordered by a concrete slab. To get up on the barn's roof, I use a shaky stepladder from the 1930s. There's a half century's worth of "stuff" piled around the barn, so there isn't really enough room to open the stepladder. We just lean it awkwardly against the roof. Yes, this scenario has danger written all over it, but when you're wearing a veil, you feel invincible, and ignore the writing.

That fateful day, I scampered up the stepladder, as much as one can scamper up a shaky stepladder while wearing a bulky suit and carrying all sorts of equipment.

To get to the high hives, I must travel 15 feet across a sloped roof and another 15 feet across a flat roof. There are three hives perched on the very edge of the flat roof. Sure, Dad and I considered positioning the hives back a bit for my safety, but thought maybe the bees would like living on the edge. After all, Dad and I do. Did I mention the rickety 1930s stepladder?

The hives were very active, always a happy sign! I placed a feeder inside each hive, which got me plenty of unwanted attention from the winged honeys. Sure, I should have smoked the bees to calm them down a bit, but the smoker

My octogenarian father often sat in his lawn chair and watched me work bees on the roof, although sometimes he did it with his eyes closed.

This photo, taken when we first set up the hives, shows a white feeder box on the top. My helper Taylor used a hive tool for several minutes to fish out most of the bees that jumped in.

that Dad and I had spent 15 minutes getting going had died as soon as I got to the hives. Relighting it would require a second treacherous trip across the barn roof. As bees pinged my veil in an increasingly aggressive fashion, I became increasingly grateful for my protective suit.

Putting the feeders in the hives was only half the work. It was now time to fill them with sugar syrup. These hives were a bit light on winter stores. Providing the bees syrup would allow them to round-out their stores if they felt the need.

Remember that expression "like bees to honey?" There's a parallel saying "like bees to sugar syrup." They love that stuff.

The syrup being poured out of plastic jugs really caught the bees' attention. Too many of them moved in for a closer look, and ended up swimming in it.

I never want to kill a single bee. I'm particularly sensitive about it in the fall, when the number of bees starts to decline, even without me accidentally drowning them. Given the option of swimming in dessert or just nibbling the edges, I'd also dive in, so I understand why the feeder was soon full of both syrup and bees.

I spent several minutes trying to save every bee swimming in the thick liquid. I dipped out probably 40; 41 had gone in. While rescuing the 41st bee, three more became submerged. This would go on until winter arrived. I finally closed the feeder lid, sacrificing a few bees. Sorry, ladies.

Remember, I'm also a klutz. While fishing out bees, I managed to get syrup all over me. Therefore, I now also had bees all over me.

With dozens of bees investigating the drops on my suit, I walked slowly across the flat barn roof, and then began the descent down the sloped portion, ever so carefully. Gravity is a wonderful thing, but sometimes it pulls me toward the concrete a bit too quickly.

Dad stood at the bottom of the stepladder, prepared to take the equipment from me. Noticing the cloud of bees about me though, he began backing away.

"Don't worry," I assured him. (Easy for me to say. I was inside a bee suit and 200 frantic-for-syrup honeybees were outside it, where Dad was.)

Oops. Maybe not all of the bees were outside. The bee walking in front of my right eye was, I think, truly right in front of my eye.

"Dad," I shakily pointed to my face with a sticky gloved finger, "is that bee on the inside?"

From his ever-increasing distance, Dad confirmed it was, and asked what I was going to do about it.

What was I going to do about it?! Wait, who is the parent here?! What happened to the hero of my childhood, my daddy who saved me from giant spiders, barking dogs and the monsters who lived in the closet?!

I was stunned that my dad wasn't going to help, and even more stunned that there was a bee in my bonnet. To heck with my usual slow steps down the last few feet of the steeper roof. I raced to the rickety stepladder. When you have a "bee in your bonnet," that's the only thing on your mind.

In record time I got off the roof, down the stepladder and out of my suit, all without being stung. I'm not sure how I did it, but it was "the bees' knees!"

Most of the time, when you're in a protective suit, you feel invincible.

But when you're sharing it with a bee...

 © 2014 Charlotte Hubbard | www.hubbardhive.com

Why We Really Remodeled the House

When our final little bird flew the nest, Hubby designed an addition that would double the size of our home.

Our house was 2200 square feet before doubling. With all kids out of the nest (except for holidays), I didn't see the logic in having twice as much floor space to vacuum. But then, there had been a couple times in decades of wedded bliss that Hubby and I disagreed. Hmm, make that a couple thousand.

My late husband wanted to double the size of the house because he said we would need the space. He cited such advantages as it would allow me to finally have a room to store all my craft stuff, and, we could have a bee room.

"We" could have a bee room? There is no "we" in bee! At the time of the house update, beekeeping was strictly his hobby. Mine was collecting yarn and fabric I couldn't live without and would someday get around to using. Really, I will.

"We don't need a bee room," I countered. "The kids' bedrooms are empty 50 weeks of the year. If you need a bee room, use one of their bedrooms. They'll be super-motivated to stay in college and focus on their studies if we fill their rooms with stinging insects."

"You don't understand," Hubby retorted, "bee rooms aren't for bees. It's for equipment. Bees don't come in the house!"

You beekeepers understand how funny that is. I could triple the size of the house if I had a dollar for every bee that hitchhiked indoors on my bee suit.

My Mom was a beekeeper. Thinking back to the 70s when she kept two hives, the need for a room to store equipment was, well, bee-wildering. Mom had a smoker, a veil, and two extra frames. She'd steal a frame from each hive each year, for our personal consumption, and replace it with one of her two empty spare frames.

Hubby also had two hives. How much bee equipment could he possibly have to store?

You beekeepers—who are probably using your extractor as an end table and five-gallon honey buckets as seating because there's no place left in your house to store everything—understand how funny that is. If you only have a couple of hives, you probably don't need much room. But, when you become obsessed with this insect such that you have two hives on the way to having ten times that, the need for equipment grows faster than a spring hive in a field of flowers.

I am a perfect example of that. A year after my husband died, "his" apiary of two hives had grown to nearly 20.

And a year later, I'd even outgrown the "bee room." Yes, he had won that argument and the size of the house doubled. Thank goodness I have room for all that equipment. Er, *had* room.

I sold Hubby's car after he passed. I didn't need a second car.

I did however need more room in the garage for bee boxes.

What's a Frame?

I'm holding a shallow frame in this photo. The light pink box, that holds ten frames, is at the right of the photo. Once bees fill up the deeper hive body frames for their consumption and use, beekeepers add shallower boxes (and frames) for even easier removal—for our consumption. Behind me is a hive with two grey boxes for the bees' stores, and a lilac box that I hoped they'd fill for humans.

Many beekeepers use a standard hive configuration called a *Langstroth*. A major advantage of this style is its easily removable frames.

Of course, easily removable frames are a major advantage for the beekeeper. The bees are generally not thrilled at how easily their hard work may be stolen.

Langstroth hives typically hold eight or ten frames per hive box (called a hive body). In the Midwest, a colony needs two or three boxes (20-30 frames) of honey to get through the winter.

 © 2014 Charlotte Hubbard | www.hubbardhive.com

Halloween

I think everyone should keep bees. There is a swarm of reasons why it is a wonderful thing. Solving the Halloween costume dilemma is one of them. Thanks to beekeeping, I now have so many options.

For example, if it is a balmy Halloween night, I wear the somewhat risqué Queen Bee costume my late husband purchased for me. Yes, it is a bit skimpy. The same could be said for the candy bars I hand out.

I feel the skimpy Queen Bee outfit is okay, as it provides an important message for kids—that bees are generous, giving-of-sweets creatures.

But, while wearing it, I've also received a few suggestive comments and looks from kids' fathers. I think it provides an important message for guys also: look if you want, but I have a stinger!

Balmy Halloween evenings are few and far between in Michigan. Thanks to beekeeping, I'm prepared for even the chilliest of them. My baggy protective bee suit lets me wear plenty of sweaters underneath, and its vivid whiteness makes me highly visible. Safety first, whether I'm stealing sweet honey from bees, or handing out sweets to little pirates.

Some of you may be wondering why this grown-up needs a Halloween costume. After all, aren't the takers of treats supposed to be the ones in costume, and not the givers?

I started wearing a costume when handing out candy about a decade ago because of an incident that intimidated me. A carload of trick-or-treaters pulled into the drive, and the kids piled out to trick-or-treat, as did the driver. I'm fairly brave, but when six towering teenagers demand candy, I tend to give it to them. Ever since then, I've worn a costume; it makes me feel a bit braver.

Wearing a bee suit helps me feel invincible in the apiary, and also in the driveway on Halloween. That first Halloween I wore it, a kid, er, a 30-year-old kid got in my face and said the two fun-sized candy bars I gave him weren't enough fun. As a lover of chocolate, I totally agree.

But from behind the zipped hood of my protective bee suit, I've faced 50,000 crazed, stinging insects. Buddy—your demands for more candy, without so much as even a "please?" Not going to happen. My driveway, my rules.

Like almost all the other trick-or-treaters a fraction of his age, this guy got only two fun-sized bars. Trick-or-treaters dressed like adorable honeybees got all they wanted.

Beekeeping can, when things go wrong, provide a third type of "costume" for Halloween. One fall, I took two stings to the left of my nose on October 29th. Thanks to an extreme, localized reaction, by the time Halloween rolled around my left eye was swollen completely shut, my right eye a mere slit, and my jaw line drooped nearly to my waistline. A couple people, not realizing that it was all natural, commented on my unbelievable make-up job. It was such a realistic ghoul appearance that I considered taking a couple intentional stings to the face every year for Halloween. By the time the anti-inflammatory medication had worn off though, I realized there were easier, more enjoyable ways to get a really fat face.

Like by eating bags of fun-sized candy bars.

From left to right, Michelle the witch, the late Tom, Charlotte, and our son Caesar, aka Ben.

Bigfoot is a Beekeeper

Remember, you read it here first.

One summer I spent two blissful hours marking queens at my out-apiary, located on my Dad's fruit and vegetable farm, which is bee heaven.

You veteran beekeepers are probably thinking "Wow, she spent two hours marking queens? She must have dozens of hives. You can mark a lot of queens in two hours."

Well, maybe *you* can.

I cannot. My "two hours of marking queens" consists of 118 minutes of looking for queens, and two minutes total dotting them.

About Marking Queens

Beekeepers may mark queens for a variety of reasons. Because the queen bee won't wear a crown, doggone it, the mark makes this one essential bee easier to spot in a hive of maybe 50,000 bees.

When you have a marked queen in a hive, and later can't find her, you'll then know that the colony either swarmed or replaced the queen (which

they'll do if she's not producing as expected). Of course, it could mean that she's also hiding REALLY well. All events warrant keeping a closer eye on that colony.

You mark a bee by holding it gently and placing a color dot on its back. The color represents the year the insect emerged, and there's a saying to help us remember what color should be used:

What: a white dot
You: a yellow dot
Raise: a red dot
Green: a green dot
Bees? : a blue dot

One method is to gently trap the queen with this little cage, and dot her. After the paint dries, the cage is removed and the queen scampers off.

Rarely does a queen bee live more than five years, so the color cycle repeats.

I've repeatedly told worker bees that if they'd flag the queen for me, I'd be in and out of their hives so much faster. (Of course, if bees were going to do what I wanted, there are a few things higher up my wish list, like "no stinging.")

In the two hours I was in and around the, embarrassingly, just—um—eight hives, the bees were seemingly as content as I was. No one buzzed loudly or even considered chasing me to the car, which has occasionally happened. After closing up the final hive, I shed my protective clothing and drove off with a big, contented smile on my face.

Dad spent many summer afternoons during his last few years, surveying what he called his personal "Garden of Eden."

I stopped by the farmhouse to visit my octogenarian father. He was busy solving the world's problems under a sprawling maple tree in the backyard—or maybe just cat-napping. His face matched my smile as I made my way across the yard to see him. "Bees must be doing well," he commented, "I can see you're happy."

My smile didn't last long. I disturbed a honeybee in the lawn, and she flew into my sandal and nailed my right foot. I launched myself into the empty chair near Dad and removed the stinger, biting my tongue. Dad might be in his 80s, but he'd still wash out my mouth with soap if I'd said aloud what I was thinking.

After the initial stinging pain subsided, Dad and I were able to laugh at the irony. I'd just worked a quarter million bees without any issues, and then got stung on an innocent stroll across the backyard.

Laughing was about the only reasonable option. I dreaded what lay ahead, but knew there wasn't much that could be done about it. The venom would run its course, and it'd be the only thing running. I'd be spending the next few days slowly hobbling on a foot swollen to the size of Miami.

> My bees were generally doing quite well, except for that particular one.

Dad and I continued to discuss bees. I still loved the furry amber insects, and Dad was right. My bees were generally doing quite well, except for that particular one. (Honeybees die after they sting.)

Within a couple of hours, I had two big toes on my right foot, the "new" big toe being the one formerly known as the little toe.

Twelve hours later, even with ice and elevation, my foot and ankle were so puffy that it was painful to walk. Luckily it was the weekend, and I took the hint and found a couch and the remote control.

While channel-surfing, which can be done on just one foot, I wandered across a "scientific" documentary on Bigfoot. This tall, hairy creature is said to inhabit the woods of the Pacific Northwest, where it enjoys salmon, berries, and (gasp!) honey. There have been very, very few sightings of this shy critter. The few times it has been seen, it lopes away. However, some short runs of its huge footprints have been found over the years. The enormous prints, for which the critter is named, have been as large as two feet long, and eight inches wide.

I looked at my swollen foot, nearing eight inches wide. And hadn't I loped awkwardly across my Dad's yard when it happened?

Perhaps there really isn't a Bigfoot species wandering the Pacific Northwest, but instead just some tall, shy, honey-loving guys living off the land who lack shoes, razors and protective suits. When they rob honey they get stung a lot, especially on their feet. That'd explain where the really big footprints come from, and because the swelling would gradually subside—that'd explain why only some footprints have been found.

Bigfoot mystery solved. Perhaps next I'll solve the mystery of where queen bees hide when you open a hive to look for them.

Cuddled to Death

When nieces Sydney and Samantha were ages four and six, one of their young playmates lost her mother to cancer.

My sister and her husband Jim sat down with Syd and Sam, and tried to explain to them the unexplainable—that sometimes people die early.

The girls studied their dad as he delivered this information, wide-eyed and solemn. Jim assured them that their parents were working hard to stay healthy (eating vegetables!) and visiting the doctor regularly, so nothing was probably going to happen to them for a long, long time.

Relieved, six-year-old Samantha scampered off to play.

Four-year-old Sydney simply sat there, staring at them. After a lengthy pause, she broke the silence with a cold "Really, Dad? Or so you think."

Jim was initially amused, but also a bit haunted. We never know what lies over the next hill. For a while, Jim wondered if his four-year-old knew something about his life span that the rest of us did not. It's been a few years now though, so his premature death is not likely to happen, or so he thinks.

Syd's stone-cold, "Or so you think," has served as a family punch line ever since. It's a classic retort to phrases such as:

"Dinner will be ready at six." (Or so you think.)

"Mom, this is the guy I want to marry." (Or so you think.)

"The dog will be fine outside of his crate." (Or so you think.)

I thought of Sydney's comment recently when I was pondering my role in my household, aka—my "hive." Beyond any question, I am the household's queen bee.

Or so I think.

Hmmm. Upon thinking about it, I'm not so sure.

In a colony of honeybees, there are three main kinds of bees. There's the all-important queen, the only bee who can lay fertile eggs and the future of the colony. She's waited on hand and foot, er, leg and leg and leg and leg and leg and leg. She doesn't lead a glamorous life though. She gets out of the hive to go on glorious mating flights only early in her life, and then must stay inside and lay eggs—1,500 to 2,000 daily during the season. To keep her focused, the worker bees take care of all her other needs.

A typical frame containing lots of worker bees, a few drones, and the all-important queen.

There are the male bees, who live to mate with a queen bee. The mating act, should they be so lucky to be chosen, results in their death. If they aren't "lucky" enough to be chosen, they're fed until mating season is over, after which most of them are kicked out to die in the cold. Until then though, they are also attended by the worker bees, who feed them, help them find the remote control, and pick up the wet towels they leave on the floor.

Worker bees, the vast majority of bees in the hives, have duties like gathering and preparing food, feeding the queen, the young bees and the drones, and cleaning up the hive. All the work falls on them.

When I thought about the roles of honeybees in a colony—maybe I'm not the queen bee.

I share a hive with two cats who only move from the front of a sunny window long enough to eat, Shiloh, the dog whom I let out (and in) 4,000 times daily, and the occasional visiting (grown-up) child who greets me with a laundry bag, and then a hug. As my days consist of activities like gathering and preparing food, and cleaning—I must be a worker bee.

There are times, though, when I feel more like a queen bee. Recently, after a long day away, I returned home. No, regretfully I hadn't been out on a mating flight. I'd been delayed at work and was now tired and crabby.

Part of the crabbiness was due to hunger. When I dashed out that morning, I'd accidentally left the lunch I packed on the kitchen counter. That lunch had included an awesome chicken salad sandwich.

Upon walking into the kitchen, I found my lunch sack shredded on the floor. Gee. I wonder who did that? Maybe the critters staring at me innocently? The three critters with chicken salad breath?

The critters then leaned against my ankles, herding me toward their still-full food bowls. Normally I feed the critters in the morning and then again late afternoon. Because they'd filled their tummies with my awesome chicken salad sandwich, they hadn't touched the food in their dishes. In their little brains though, it was time to be fed.

Or so I thought. Perhaps they weren't herding me toward their feeding dishes. Perhaps they were trying to get rid of me.

You see, when a honeybee colony is preparing to swarm, the old queen leaves the hive. But before she can, they need to thin her down so she can fly. They do this by withholding food (eating her lunch?) and chasing her about the hive. The animals did seem to want to keep me moving. Maybe they were just helping me shed those few extra pounds. They certainly know a lot about shedding—of fur, anyway.

The old queen bee swirling off in a swarm is only one way a colony might get rid of her. Sometimes, they simply kill her.

I snuggled on the couch to read more about queen bee replacement. Shiloh hopped up on the couch where she's never allowed, and curled up at my feet. Chloe the shy kitten posed as a meatloaf on my shoulder, her purr the best relaxation music one could hear. Melvin the obese cat settled his enormousness

 © 2014 Charlotte Hubbard | www.hubbardhive.com

on my lungs, making it hard to breathe. One of the glorious advantages of pets is that they warm up humans quite nicely, although the three of them were making me a bit toasty.

Perhaps too toasty.

Reading about queen bee replacement made my blood run cold. Based on the reading, I believe I'm the queen bee in my hive, and I believe I'm in trouble: I read, "Worker bees may choose to kill the current queen by clustering tightly around her until she dies from overheating, often called 'cuddle death.'"

No, it can't be. My hive mates aren't thinking of replacing me, their queen bee, are they? They are just being affectionate, snuggly, and friendly—right?

Or so I think.

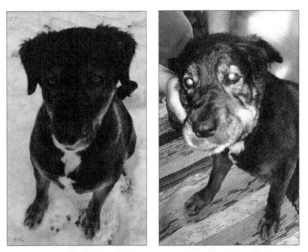

Shiloh usually has a sensitive, slender face. Although after a few stings from getting too close to a hive, that sensitive face can really swell.

My Favorite Things About Bees

Whenever someone asks why I keep bees, I tend to give a typical answer like, "Because they're critical to human survival and need our help."

You see, non-beekeepers don't understand the real reason I have a full-sized freezer dedicated to honeycomb, not ice cream (freezing honeycomb kills wax moths). They're confused as to why I park outside all winter (because the garage is full of equipment). They think I keep bees for their honey, because they can't understand being head-over-hive tool in love with a stinging insect.

I can live without ice cream, maybe. I don't want to live without bees.

Yes, I know it's odd, but that's the way it is. I can live without ice cream, maybe. I don't want to live without bees.

I immensely enjoy the things bees create, like honey and blueberries. I enjoy the insects themselves even more. Here are some of my favorite things about them.

Exoskeletons: I was flabbergasted the first time I saw a beekeeper simply flick a hundred bees off the face of a comb—amazed at how beekeepers can just do that, amazed at the light click of bees bouncing off top bars, and amazed at how bees are seemingly not bothered by it. If you brush me off a surface 20 times my height, well, perhaps I've had too much ice cream. It won't be a light

click when I land.

I'm also a little envious of bees' exoskeletons. Having one sure would be handy when I bang into all that equipment in the garage.

Expressive faces: I love opening a hive to find a line of inquisitive bees peeking at me. I want to believe they're just curious, although I've found that their innocent expressions hide an intense search for an opening in my bee suit.

 © 2014 Charlotte Hubbard | www.hubbardhive.com

Pollen baskets: Every time I struggle to pull on my just-laundered jeans, I'm envious that bees can simply remove the bulges from their thighs. And what beautiful bulges they are—buttery yellow, sweet pink, pearl white and even lime green.

Dancing: As a college freshman, near a free-flowing keg at the fraternity, I spent more than one evening dancing with wild abandon, certain that it was purposeful and beautiful.

I wish my thighs looked that good.

The drinking age was raised from 18 to 21 shortly thereafter. Coincidence? Perhaps. Nonetheless, being underage, plus my struggle with higher mathematics, curtailed most of my drinking the next few years.

Compared to bees, my dance was not, nor has ever been, either purposeful or beautiful. The bees' ability to communicate mathematical concepts with dance—like the distance to blossoms, and where they are relative to the hive, is even more humbling. Bees, I raise my glass to you. Yes, I can legally drink now. Love the mead, by the way.

Our shared, tender moments—the ones that turned out well: One of the downsides of beekeeping is the encounters that didn't turn out well. I don't remember the stings so much as the magical moments that did go well—like when one of you landed on my arm during a child's graduation, and again as I stood on a busy sidewalk in Washington D.C. I was honored to be your refuge.

Another such mystical time was at my out-apiary. Honey bees thrive in that wooded area, as do ticks. Late September, while checking a hive, I felt something crawling up my face.

Initially I was grossed out by thoughts of a tick wandering about my cheek. But when I lowered my eyes and instead gazed into the insect's multiple, compound eyes, and then at its translucent wings and raised stinger-end, I wished it had been a tick. Having a bee on the same side of the protective suit as me usually doesn't end well for either of us.

> *A bee on the same side of the protective suit as me usually doesn't end well for either of us.*

But, that sweet bee did nothing as I held my breath, except walk all over my face with an amazingly strong grip. I ever-so-carefully removed my veil, and a few long minutes later, she flew off.

Delighted, I've told several humans about that encounter. For a few moments, I connected with a little lady from the insect world. I hope that worker bee also felt our connection, and spent the winter clustered with her sisters, telling them about the magic of inter-species bonding.

But I suspect the conversation in the hive was instead something like this:

"They have no exoskeleton! And simple eyes, only two of them! They have huge pollen baskets they can't unload."

"But my favorite thing about humans is getting under the veil. It really freaks them out. Come closer, I'll tell you how. We'll have so much fun with them come spring!"

 © 2014 Charlotte Hubbard | www.hubbardhive.com

Pictorial of the Honey Process

One of everyone's favorite things about honeybees is honey!

It begins with beautiful flowers, which lure honeybees with their sweet scent of nectar.

In the process of collecting nectar, bees brush against pollen, and then carry that pollen to other similar plants—pollination!

Bees practice "flower fidelity"—pollinating all dogwood for a bit, then all dandelions, etc. That instinctive behavior ensures that pollen is transferred to comparable plants. Otherwise, there might be such things as doglions. ☺

The bees working in the field, called foragers, collect nectar in what is called a "honey stomach."

If you're wondering how that nectar gets out of the honey stomach, think about it. Well, don't think too much, because yes, you guessed it. One of the most wonderful things we humans enjoy is—bee barf.

When the forager bees return to the hive, they regurgitate the nectar directly into the honey stomachs of other worker bees. These "processor bees" have the job of processing that nectar.

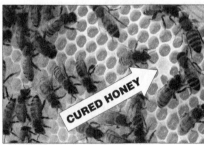

The processor bees, with their honey stomachs full of nectar, move to the appropriate honeycomb location. There they regurgitate the nectar into hexagonal wax cells.

Each regurgitation adds an enzyme to the nectar. That enzyme further breaks down the nectar into simpler sugars.

Once the honey reaches the right

These processor honeybees are working the honey-to-be—patrolling, checking cell integrity, and filling honeycomb cells, which requires multiple regurgitations.

moisture level, or becomes "cured," the bees cover it with a wax cap. Once cured, the honey contains such little water that microbes are unable to grow in it, preventing it from becoming contaminated by bacteria or fungi. Cured honey, appropriately stored, lasts forever.

How does honey go from hive to your tummy?

While commercial beekeepers have massive, automated extraction equipment, we hobbyists have a more manual process.

After we've robbed the frames of capped honey from the hives (a process that often involves smoke, some unhappy bees, and invariably, the hottest weather of the year), we slice off that beautiful wax cap the bees had put on each cell (top photo).

Those frames are then loaded into the extractor (center), where they're spun. Centrifugal force removes most of the honey from each cell.

We then open the gate and the honey pours through a couple of filters into a bucket (lower photo), from which we fill bottles and bears.

It's a labor-intensive, sticky process, but a labor of love.

 © 2014 Charlotte Hubbard | www.hubbardhive.com

My Drone

As noted in the first essay, by the time my late husband Tom saw a doctor for his health issues, he was told he only had months to live.

Tom's body had been screaming that something was dreadfully wrong for over a year, but he hadn't listened to it. He certainly wasn't going to listen to oncologists with decades of experience who told him he wouldn't be around much longer either.

I hated Tom's stubbornness. And although stubbornness killed him, it's also a key reason why he lived 18 months instead of the handful the doctors predicted. And he wrung all the life he could from those 18 months.

Stubbornness being the most predominant of Tom's many strong personality characteristics, I don't know if he ever really considered that he might die of cancer. Fortunately, the disease shut down his brilliant mind just before it claimed its final victory. I don't believe Tom ever had an awareness that it was just about over.

But, the knowledge that he likely would be dying prematurely framed many of my thoughts for 18 months. When Tom was fighting infections, I thought about how I would probably be a widow sooner rather than much, much later. When stoplights or the line at the grocery stole long minutes away from the fleeting time we might have together, I couldn't help but think that someday I'd likely be shopping for one. Every time Tommy and I enjoyed a dazzling sunset and life seemed absolutely perfect, I was fighting hard to stay in the moment and not worry about the next day or the next test result.

In the darkest hours of many sleepless nights, I would occasionally think about the future. I certainly wouldn't be the first to lose a spouse; it was survivable. I'd probably even someday find another person who could elbow me at night when I snored.

Some folks might be critical that I let my thoughts wander to life after Tom while he still lived. No apologies folks. I'm glad it happened. For me, peering into that horrendous abyss before I actually got to it made navigating it when I got there a little easier.

Just over a year after Tommy died, I began dating again. I dreaded it, but did want to find someone with whom I could share my life. Our kids had moved out and on with theirs. My dog, two cats, and half-million bees were great companions, but not easy to take to a movie. Getting gussied up and getting out to meet strangers was hard, but it needed to be done. There were possibly hundreds of dates, personal heartaches and broken hearts before I found the next Mr. Charlotte. I might as well get started.

Having not dated in 30+ years, I was unsure how to even go about it. Friends urged me to try online dating. I reluctantly, cautiously did.

I thought a great deal about the requirements I listed on the dating website.

I'm tall. Assuming I had years of dating ahead of me, I wanted to wear heels at least a few times. Feeling a little shallow, I specified guys who I could look up to, 6'2" or taller.

I pondered listing "must love honeybees" but feared that would really narrow my dating options. Many folks don't understand why anyone would keep bees. And honestly, every time I'm lifting a heavy box of honey in 90 degree heat with 40,000 bees telling me they're not happy about it, even I wonder why I keep honeybees.

Six months later—February 2011—found me dating many tall men who matched my criteria, but whom I could tell, after just one date, I'd never bring home to meet the pets.

One day, as I was reviewing yet even more potential dates, the site suggested someone who met most of my criteria. Marshall was only 6', but he was local and had also lost his spouse. By the way, that expression of "losing" someone always makes me chuckle. It's not like I misplaced Tom under some papers and he might show up at any time.

That's probably good, because it'd be awkward. You see, I said yes to meeting Marshall. His living only a few miles away meant it would be convenient to have coffee. Because he was widowed, for a change I wouldn't have to hear about someone's ex who divorced him just because he was playing video games when he wasn't golfing.

Marshall and I met on a Saturday morning. It wasn't love at first sight, but there was something there, so much so that I canceled my other two upcoming dates that weekend to explore what it might be.

That "something there" grew. I appreciated that Marshall didn't play video games endlessly, or golf for that matter. Like me, he loved long winter walks in the woods with the dog. And yes, I let him meet the dog. She and I are inseparable.

My bees and I are also inseparable, but I didn't want to share them with just anyone. As they were snug in hives for the winter instead of begging for attention with gentle brown eyes at my feet, it was easy not to tell Marshall anything about them. Nor would I, until I was sure he was worthy. Every time we went out to walk in the woods, I'd divert his attention from the pink, green and light blue boxes poking out of the snowdrifts in the corner of the yard.

We took one such walk on a sunny day in late February. This beekeeper's eye saw the numerous brown spots in the snow, and I smiled. That meant there were bees alive, and they were relieving themselves outside the hive. Glory bee!

I wanted to see which hives had activity, as well as kiss the shiny wings of all the bees I saw and celebrate their survival. After a few seconds of hesitation, I steered Marshall to the hives. We stopped about ten feet away and watched dozens of bees joyfully zipping about in the fresh air. Surprisingly, he took his eyes off *me* for a change and seemed equally enthralled by the bees' merriment.

I didn't say much more about my bees. If he didn't get how I felt about them by my mile-wide smile, he probably figured it out when I did awkward cartwheels in snow boots.

Unfortunately, many of those hives alive in February were no longer around by March, but Marshall still was. My feelings for him grew deeper when he helped lug the hives into the garage, and spent his day off cleaning up dead-outs with me.

April arrived, and so did packages of bees to expand my apiary. Putting road-weary bees into a hive can be a crazy event, but Marshall calmly helped install them. He was also interested in checking their progress a week later, and enthusiastically helped build frames and paint boxes for the growing colonies. It appeared that he really, really liked bees, and possibly me as well.

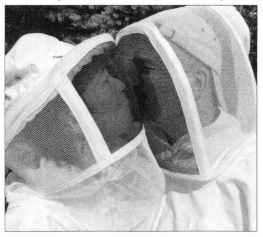
Here we are working bees together.

My first husband's parents were my parents-in-law for decades; their opinion remains important to me. In telling them about Marshall, I shared that another point in his favor was that he even liked bees.

"Some guys," chuckled my father-in-law, "will do anything to get the girl."

That opinion made me a bit nervous. Part of me had been wondering if Marshall was really interested in me, or if I was just a bridge to his real true love—honeybees. Time would tell.

In time, Marshall took his share of rookie stings. He was itchy and puffy, but still enthused.

More time passed. We pulled honey, and he liked hanging out with me, even when I was in a sweat-soaked bee suit.

As summer rolled along, we counted parasitic mites in the hives together. We assembled more frames for colonies quickly outgrowing their hives, and extracted honey. By August he could read a hive as quickly as I could. We had long discussions about the future of a few weak hives, and somewhere in all of that—discussions of our future as well.

By the end of September, after meeting the last of my brood, we decided to make it official. Time was critical in our relationship. Fall is when you get rid of any unwanted drones before they drain winter stores. I'd made the decision that this drone was worth keeping around.

In October, Marshall removed the lid of a hive and found a couple of wedding rings. Curious honeybees clambered over them.

The very private and absolutely perfect wedding venue.

 © 2014 Charlotte Hubbard | www.hubbardhive.com

I answered the stunned questioning look in his eyes. Yes, I was proposing. The queen bee is really in charge of everything.

A few weeks later, in the corner of my Dad's vineyard not far from my, er, soon-to-be our out-apiary, we slipped on those bee-blessed rings. The ceremony was attended only by our widowed octogenarian fathers, the pastor, the dog, and this weird metal bird sculpture that shows up unexpectedly around my Dad's farm.

Southbound geese called overhead, brilliantly colored leaves fell from autumn maples, the dog chased squirrels, and the sun shone warmly, even though the morning had begun with a crisp October rain.

The bird that seemingly roams the farm, and wandered back to witness our vows in the rolling vineyard. We now have a third apiary quite near that location.

The day and the setting could not have been more perfect. The vows exchanged, including 'til death do we part, were rich and sobering in significance. I looked into the blue-grey eyes of my groom, eyes that I'd seen through a protective veil, eyes that had smiled often at me in a snowy woods, eyes that lit up during visits from our kids and romps with our dog, eyes that glittered upon seeing frames of honey.

We were united in marriage, and it felt like it was meant to bee.

This Keeping of Bees

Beekeepers come in all shapes, sizes and ages.

We use different types of equipment, approach diseases and pests with a variety of methods, and happily keep one hive as a hobby, or thousands as an occupation. (No matter how many we have, chances are we need—er, want—more.)

This is a top bar hive (TBH), an increasingly popular equipment choice. Some beekeepers suggest bees kept in TBHs are happier and healthier. TBH bees aren't necessarily larger, although that bee in the upper left of the photo looks enormous. She was as curious about the camera as we were about the inside of the TBH.

Working with bees means an inevitable sting or two, or two dozen. It happens to all of us, but we react differently. Some of us swell up like cartoon characters and itch for days—but of course that doesn't keep us from working with our bees. Some beekeepers react violently and nearly fatally to stings—but of course that doesn't keep them from working with bees. Yet others, the lucky few, aren't bugged at all by what this bug does to them.

We share some common traits and characteristics, beyond our shared, uncommon fascination (obsession) with this insect. This section explores some of them.

We _May_ Bee Prone to Exaggeration

I've been blessed to mentor several beginning beekeepers in the last few years. Mentoring comes with challenges, like helping these new-bees overcome their fear of bees, making sure they don't kill their queens, and managing unrealistic expectations (like they'll make a pile of money keeping bees). As the joke in beekeeping circles goes, "Making a small fortune as a beekeeper is easy. Just start with a large fortune."

One year I mentored a tall, lanky new-bee named David, who was encouraged by his uncle to keep bees. The uncle claimed he was making a ton of money doing it; David wanted part of that.

Despite my best efforts and a ton of ba-bee-sitting, David started his first year of beekeeping with ten hives, but ended up with only six. Undaunted, he planned to add 24 the next season.

I told him that seemed a bit aggressive, and asked his reasons.

"Payback," he explained. "My uncle told me he averaged 300 pounds of honey per hive last year. If I can get that from my hives, I can buy a new truck."

I gently shared with David that 300 pounds of honey per hive was, well, very impressive.

"You don't think my uncle is exaggerating, do you?" David asked indignantly.

Quite frankly, yes I did. But having never met the man, I was hesitant to accuse him.

And because I never met the man, I did have a bit of a bee in my bonnet about this uncle in the bee business. He was the one who got his nephew into beekeeping, yet I was the one who had shown David how to assemble a frame. I was the one who had gone out on a literal limb to help David capture his colony that swarmed. I was the one sweating with him in August as we searched for a queen in a very angry (and as it turned out, queenless) hive.

"Look at what other beekeepers report," I suggested. "300 pounds seems a bit high. But as your uncle's been keeping bees for 30 years, maybe he has secret tricks."

Inwardly I chuckled to myself. I've met these wizened beekeepers with gray beards down to their navels. They lay claim to smokers that burn for days on end, queens that are prolific for decades, hives that average 300 pounds a year. I'm not saying they're lying, but I'd be lying if I said I thought they were telling the truth.

I've only been a beekeeper for a handful of years, but I have noticed that beekeepers are prone to exaggeration.

I once went to a summer bee event. Because the temperature was hovering around 120 degrees Fahrenheit, I took a break under an oak tree with limbs a mile wide. A hundred or so of these wizened beekeepers were already cooling themselves there, two of them deep in a conversation that I couldn't help but overhear.

A swarm, but probably not a 100,000 bee swarm.

"Great year for swarms," mentioned the first, running a calloused hand down six feet of coarse gray beard. "I caught three in one day."

"Just three?" spit out the second. "I had five one day, and turned the phone off so I wouldn't get any more calls."

"I had to quit answering the phone after the third swarm," countered the first beekeeper. "It must've had 100,000 bees in it. Took me several boxes to capture it."

"Yeah, I've seen a few swarms that size," rejoined the second. "But most of mine this year were at least twice that big."

"Don't care about how big they are as long as they produce," countered the first beekeeper. "Last year I got so much honey off one hive that it paid for my new bass boat all by itself."

"You fish for bass?" the second beekeeper shook his head slowly. "I had to stop. Hurt my back pulling out a 60-pounder. Miss it, but it gives me more time for bees. Takes a bit of time when you've got a thousand hives to manage like I got, and I work them all by myself."

He did not have the body of a man who worked a thousand hives. The buttons of his shirt hadn't met the holes in years.

I took a second glance at this man. He did not have the body of a man who worked a thousand hives. The buttons of his shirt hadn't met the holes in years. As I was eavesdropping though, perhaps I didn't hear that conversation quite right.

You see, my hearing just hasn't been the same, ever since I captured those 200-pound swarms. Seven of them, all in one day.

Go Blue

Beekeeping has many labor-intensive aspects. Beyond the actual keeping of bees, you can also spend vast amounts of time extracting and bottling honey, building and repairing equipment, and painting hives. And, if you're like me, you can spend most of the summer looking for your hive tool. A hive tool is an inexpensive but essential slender piece of metal that allows you to easily pry open a hive, remove the frames, or pierce the seat of your car.

Recently, I put fresh coats of paint on many of our hives. As I applied orange paint to my hands, jeans, shoes, dog and even occasionally the hive, I thought about how non-beekeepers often ask, "Aren't hives supposed to be white?"

No, hives aren't required to be white. In fact, they aren't even required to be painted. We do paint ours though, to both protect the wood and to enhance their appearance. Plus, the few weeks of the dog wagging her paint-streaked tail always makes me smile.

We knew the colleges had money. After all, we were steadily writing checks to them.

Many folks, when they see our rainbow of hives, are surprised they aren't all white. I understand their confusion. Growing up, I also thought all bees live in white hives. In the children's literature I devoured, the hives were always white. Sure, my glasses were thicker than the pile of books I read by flashlight under the covers at night, but I could still see colors accurately.

Decades later, I read different story books to my children. The hives pictured in those books were always white too.

Of course, story books can be deceptive. In those stories, happy beekeepers were surrounded by just a couple equally smiley bees, instead of hundreds of crazed insects. There also were no parasitic mites decimating the country's bee population. But there were other threats—like bears sporting funny hats and striped pants who steal honey—or that wild, honey-stealing Winnie-the-Pooh who doesn't even wear pants.

Now then, about deciding what color to paint hives...

When my late husband Tom began keeping bees, he read that light, pastel

 © 2014 Charlotte Hubbard | www.hubbardhive.com

colors were preferred. He painted one of his first two hives a subtle lilac, and the other a warm, golden honey color. Coincidentally, those are about the colors of our local school system.

Tom increased his apiary to five colonies the following year, and thus, had three more hives to paint. He selected colors representing where our two oldest kids were attending college—adding orange and light blue to the apiary—along with a pink.

People couldn't help notice our apiary was starting to look like a tropical fishing village, and became curious. Tom jokingly explained we were painting hives to match the kids' college colors (plus pink), in the hopes that maybe someday, when the apiary became famous, the colleges would pay a small fee to have their logo painted on the hive. We knew the colleges had money. After all, we were steadily writing checks to them.

In due time, we added a second U of M hive. They did quite well—notice the number of boxes on them indicating how much room they needed. The hive on the right is "bearding", a fun term beekeepers use to describe what happens when the foragers return from the field in the late afternoon, and don't want to go inside where it is warm and crowded. Sometimes you see them playing cards or enjoying icy tropical drinks.

Speaking of colors, the next year was bright red in our family budget. Due to poor family planning, we'd reached the point in our life when we'd have two kids in college and a third in bank-account-draining grad school. Our extra dollars were few and far between. But, our baby was going to college. It was family tradition now for there to be a hive of her collegiate colors.

"Luckily" our baby selected the University of Michigan, where her big brother was also attending. I say "luckily" because there was already a hive painted the appropriate color (Go Blue!) We didn't have to purchase more bees and equipment, AND, we could now send both their tuition payments with just one stamp. When you have two kids in college and a third in bank-account-draining grad school, you'll pinch the pennies wherever you can.

Our kids are all through college now, so I can select whatever colors move me. This year's hives are a cherry red, honey gold, and hunter orange. I selected those colors because the paint smears look really good on my jeans, and the dog's tail.

30,000 Tiny Winter Coats

My late husband Tom was absolutely delighted to keep bees, and would talk about them with anyone who was interested (or not!) for hours.

People assumed that because Tom was a beekeeper, he knew a lot about bees, and would ask him all sorts of questions. One of his most favorite questions was asked of him three minutes into trying to order dinner. The waiter, whom we'd just met, inquired about the bee pin on my jacket; Tom answered that we were beekeepers.

Tom knew a lot about bees, but disappointingly, did not know that answer.

"Beekeepers?!" said the waiter, forgetting the day's specials to chat insects instead. "I have so many questions. Like that sting my nephew got while playing baseball—was that a honeybee?"

Tom knew a lot about bees, but disappointingly, did not know that answer.

Tom and I loved studying our colorful hives when they were active. Neighbors who wandered by would wonder what we were looking at, and ended up joining us in watching the hundreds of takeoffs and landings. Inevitably, they'd ask, "How do the bees know which hive is theirs?"

The answer involves orientation flights and role of pheromones, but what fun is that? Tom's ready answer was "we give them little T-shirts that match their hive color."

One questioner, who holds a position of significant responsibility in the medical field, then asked, "They wear T-shirts?"

Seconds later, realizing what a ridiculous question she'd asked, she blushed a deep, deep red. Her face would've matched an Ohio State or Wisconsin hive, but those aren't allowed in an apiary sporting hives painted to salute the University of Michigan.

Another question Tom was always asked was, "Why are all the honeybees dying?"

 © 2014 Charlotte Hubbard | www.hubbardhive.com

Tom would secretly roll his eyes at that question. Researchers from all around the world with miles of credentials are trying to solve that mystery. Did people really think that Tom, backyard beekeeper, knew the answer and was just keeping it quiet?

Nonetheless, Tommy would use the opportunity to educate people about the importance of honeybees. He'd affirm that Colony Collapse Disorder (CCD) is an extremely serious issue, and would share some of the theories about the cause.

With a twinkle in his eye, he'd also offer his theory. "I think cell phones have something to do with the honeybees disappearing."

The questioners would then ponder this, sort of nod their heads, and usually say, "Really? Cell phones?"

"Yes, I think that's part of the problem," he'd answer. "That's why we don't let our bees carry them, especially when flying."

Tom's been gone a few years now, but CCD continues, as do the questions about it. When I'm asked, I must confess that I don't worry about CCD killing any bees in my apiary. For the first few years it would've been nearly impossible— they were instead dying each winter, predominantly from beekeeper error.

One of my favorite things about keeping bees is the continuing education it provides. Of course, that's also one of my least favorite things about keeping bees—the many lessons I continue to learn.

Knock on wood, my hives do better at surviving the oft-harsh Michigan winters now. It's because, come November, I give them all little winter coats.

That match the color of their hives, of course.

The Importance of a Bee Veil and Chocolate

The first time I worked bees, it was because my very ill husband Tom had, unbee-knownst to me, ordered more colonies of the stinging critters. The buzzing packages arrived at our home just days after Tom returned home from a month's hospitalization.

Tom had surgical wounds, cancer in multiple organs, and chemotherapy side effects. I had none of that, but I did have a bad attitude about stinging insects. Nonetheless, he... won? I was the one who had to "install" the bees.

"Install" is a cool beekeeping term that means get the bees into the hive (and cross your fingers they stay there). Armed with Tom's protective suit, I prepared to dump thousands of stinging bugs into their new homes, assuming they'd go in as easily as shown on the video.

Bees are shipped through the mail (yes, really) in cages like this one. Your local Post Office will really appreciate it if you pick them up as early as possible in the day.

As the bees readily demonstrate in this photo, they don't all go in the hive and stay. I guess I should have showed them the video also.

As I slipped into Tom's bee suit that (fateful) day, I recall looking at my bare ankles. I momentarily wondered if I should wear socks, but then thought "Naaah—what are the bees going to do? Fly up out of the hive after they've been dumped in, weave their way down through the tall grass and sting my ankles?"

Yes.

That was one of my first key beekeeping lessons: wear socks.

The second time I needed to work bees, I again wore Tom's too-short bee suit, and still had a bad attitude. But, I also had socks—tall, thick ones, reaching nearly to my knees. I remember thinking, "That should stop them. It's not like

 © 2014 Charlotte Hubbard | www.hubbardhive.com

they're going to fly out, weave their way down through the tall grass and then fly up my pant leg until they find bare skin, are they?"

The answer to that question is also yes. It was then I learned the VERY important lesson of tucking your pants into your socks.

I'm not sure what getting my 100th sting means and I don't think I want to know that answer.

When people share why they keep bees, a common answer is because they love learning. There is always something new to know about these insects and how to best keep them.

In the years I've been keeping bees, I've found this to be so true. In my fourth year, in late February, I learned yet another lesson.

I now own a bee suit that's long enough for me, providing an additional protective layer around the tender ankle area bees love so dearly. I also own a jacket, handy for when I don't want the added warmth or weight of a full suit.

That breezy, unseasonably sunny February day, I donned that jacket as I was already wearing jeans, tucked the jeans into my socks, and greeted one of my booming winter-surviving hives.

My late husband had always appreciated that particular pair of jeans on me. He liked their softness and how they hugged my figure.

Turns out bees really like them also, finding them easy to sting through. They nailed my thighs three times before I realized they weren't so happy to see that I had survived the winter right along with them.

Ouch. And ouch and ouch. (True confession: I yelled a different word when they stung me.)

And *&%! some more. Those stings really, well, *stung!* It was great to see bees flying in February. It was not great that they chased me for several hundred feet that unusually balmy afternoon.

As I tell beginning beekeepers, it doesn't matter how gentle, cautious, or careful you are. Stings happen.

If you're not reckless or uncoordinated like me, you can avoid most of them. But, even when I'm super careful, stings happen. Speaking from too much experience, if I had a choice about where to take a sting, the thigh is the best place. Unlike stings near the eye, thighs are easier to scratch and ice.

For the next few days, after those February stings, I dealt with my puffy, itchy thighs by holding a chocolate milkshake between them. Several milkshakes each day helped keep down the swelling, and made me feel better. Calories consumed for medicinal purposes don't count, right?

As I also tell new beekeepers: because stings do happen, you need to embrace them. Getting your first sting means you're a real beekeeper.

I'm not sure what getting my 100th sting means and I don't think I want to know that answer.

I also tell new-bees that the best way to deal with stings is to avoid getting them, which means:

1. Wear protective gear.
(I'm partial to wearing a full bee suit now. It's maximum protection, and a great way to hide that extra pound or two or twelve.)

2. Wear socks.

3. Tuck your pants into your socks.

And when those protective measures fail, have chocolate on standby.

 © 2014 Charlotte Hubbard | www.hubbardhive.com

Beekeeper Fantasies

My friend Jon, who works as a mild-mannered software nerd, has a private pilot's license. On the rare occasions Jon flies commercially, he confesses he has a secret fantasy. He hopes something (temporary) happens to the pilots. When the nervous flight attendants ask if there are any pilots onboard, Jon will step forward, safely land the plane, and be quite the (mild-mannered software nerd) hero. Jon says his fantasy is shared by almost every private pilot he knows.

I have a similar fantasy involving flying. Flying insects, that is.

Jon and I had a conversation about our hobbies' fantasies recently when I gave him a ride. Before he could climb in the car, I had to remove my long leather protective gloves and suit from the passenger seat. Jon asked why I carry bee equipment in the vehicle.

The first reason is that I have two apiaries. I was always forgetting something at the remote one, and learned the hard way that when you forgot your light-colored leather gloves, wearing black winter mittens is a bad idea. Bears are a natural enemy of bees. Evolution has trained the insects to attack anything that resembles dark, furry paws getting into their hives. And unfortunately, my mittens, that must resemble bear paws, did not cover my wrists. Ouch, ouch, ouch!

The second reason is because of what I suspect is every beekeeper's fantasy: We hope to be driving down the road, and find a crowd of people stopped because there's a huge swarm of honeybees clustered on, say, cute twin babies and a pile of really fluffy kittens. The crowd will be paralyzed with fear. We will hand our protective suit to the twins' mother. Wearing just street clothes, we will stride through the crowd and capture the swarm, putting it safely into the box we happen to also have in the car.

After the bees are secured, we will hand the unharmed twins to their mom, and pass out kittens to adorable small children who will be looking at us like we're super heroes. (Which beekeepers are.)

"Gee," said Jon, "I thought a beekeeper's fantasy would just involve a lot of honey."

It does. Part Two of the fantasy is when the swarm settles nicely into our apiary. It survives every winter. Every spring we have to split it into three hives because it is so strong.

Beekeepers. We're always dreaming, and we dream big.

Yes, Bees Die

BEEKEEPER'S LEARNING CURVE

They say that nothing worth doing is easily done. Keeping bees is no exception; there's a horrendous learning curve.

Whenever I meet a beekeeper, I ask what they wished they would've known in the bee-ginning. What would've helped them more quickly climb that learning curve?

I've been tracking these insightful responses for years now.[1] Some answers cause me to shake my head and silently wonder how these people managed to miss such critical, introductory information. For example, a gentleman told me sheepishly that he initially didn't recognize the importance of the queen bee[2]; nor did he realize that there is generally only one queen per hive. When he spotted this abnormally large bee with other bees clustered all over it, he thought it might be a bully or genetic freak, and killed it.

Yes, really.

Others responses are very familiar, like Sean's, who said "Why didn't anyone tell me that my bees might die, no matter what I do?! I'm beyond consolation."

That bees die wasn't news to me, and I suspect not to Sean either. What was a surprise though was how apparently easy it is to kill them. For the first few years of beekeeping, the only expertise I could claim was the ability to dependably kill my bees every winter.

Disassembling a hive full of dead bees claws at the beekeeper's soul. Years later, when speaking at a convention, I shared with the audience how emotionally tough it is to find a dead hive, even though practically every year I experience it.

A grandfatherly, bearded guy in the front row interrupted and waved his arthritic hand frantically. I called on him.

"Had bees for half my life now," his hand nervously found the pockets of his bib overalls. "Seen hundreds of dead hives. She's so right. It's awful. And you *never* get used to it."

---

1   I'd appreciate your sharing what you wish you'd known in the beginning. I welcome your insights at *queenbeecharlotte@gmail.com*.
2   She's the only bee in the colony who can lay fertilized eggs. Without the queen, the colony has no future.

My murdering thousands of innocent insects began with the best of intentions.

Late husband Tom started beekeeping in 2006 with two hives. He located them in what my uncle, a state apiary inspector, called "the absolute worst possible location on the property."

Even the best beekeepers lose bees. You have to get right back on the horse.

My uncle may have known that was the absolute worst possible location; the bees did not. Tom was very, very afraid of bees and did nothing much with them other than put them in their hives. Thus, for two years, in the absolutely worst possible location on the property, those neglected bees happily buzzed into the warm sunshine each spring to let us know that all was right with the world (other than Tom having yet undiagnosed stage IV colorectal cancer).

When the cancer was finally discovered, Tom was quite ill. I reluctantly took over beekeeping. Tom had ordered three more packages of live bees, meaning I needed a crash course on bee installation (and treating bee stings). As spring stretched into summer, my fascination grew. I read everything I could, talked with dozens of beekeepers, spent evenings surfing the internet while Tom slept.

As a result, the colonies of our apiary never went into winter so well tended. They had emergency feed, a tar paper wrap, and thick, towering wind blocks of straw bales.

Because of my hours of research and pampering, by next spring, all had died.

It turns out I had blocked too much of winter's arctic chill. Bees shiver to keep warm, and that generates moisture. Without ventilation to remove it, that moisture rises to the top of their hive, condenses, and drops down on them. Bees can handle cold, they can't handle wet and cold.

All these bees are dead, and died huddled together against the cold. The white substance on the top is sugar, placed along their ceiling as emergency feed.

The bottom of a hive that perished over a winter (after I removed the upper boxes). Bees huddle in a cluster for warmth, and as they die, they fall to the bottom.

I was nearly inconsolable. Piles of bee carcasses lined the bottom of each hive, a few hundred dead bees clutched each other of the face of honeycomb. Such a dreadful, awful, waste.

I cleaned up those five dead hives, and ordered more bees. While I questioned (and um, still question) my beekeeping skills, a senior beekeeper told me I had two key characteristics to someday be successful: curiosity, and hope. Even the best beekeepers lose bees. You have to get right back on the horse.

The next year, curiosity and hope led me to experiment with a variety of winter survival techniques. Trying to be scientific in my approach, I paired my hives at different locations, and tested only one variable per pair. I figured I'd see which hives survived where, and then use those techniques and locations the following year.

God has a grand sense of humor. That following spring, one hive of each type survived at each location. My painstaking data indicated nothing, other than that I'm as good at recording data as I am at killing bees.

There should be a support group for us hobbyists who have lost (er, killed) the very essence of our hobby. We could commiserate for a while, and then help each other get right back on the horse.

Hope springs eternal in beekeepers.

The winter of '14 in the Midwest was particularly devastating. We'd left on more honey than we usually do, but because of the winter that wouldn't leave, the bees ate it and their emergency sugar stores as well. In this photo, you can see the tails of bees deep into the honeycomb, trying to get any honey from the back wall. The brownish covering on some cells is brood. These bees were alive until mid-March; the queen had started laying again in anticipation of spring. And then there was that week of single-digit temperatures—argh!

 © 2014 Charlotte Hubbard | www.hubbardhive.com

How Can an Insect so Small Require So Much Storage Space?

When we had our first child, we lived hours away from both sets of doting grandparents.

There was plenty I didn't understand about babies, like efficient burping, the need to carry 45 extra outfits for them in the diaper bag, and how even with 2,000 pacifiers you can't find one when you need it.

I also didn't understand that roads between the grandchild and the grandparents predominantly only go one way. Sure, there were occasions when the grandparents would come to the big city and stay in our crowded, noisy apartment to coo at their grand treasure. But every holiday, we were to go to them.

That was generally OK. Did I mention our apartment was crowded and noisy?

Sometimes though, like the mornings after the little darling had been up all night, loading up and driving several hours in holiday traffic was challenging. I was always amazed at how long it took to pack the baby's essentials for a weekend, and how much stuff was required. Adults travel with only a toothbrush and a clean pair of underwear, although I've been told the latter isn't necessary, you can just turn the current pair inside out. Babies require several times their body weight in stuff. Large, cumbersome stuff.

So do bees.

When I first began keeping bees, I figured one extra box for honey, per hive was all I'd need. (Of course, I also incorrectly assumed a few hives were all I'd need, although I know now you can never have enough.)

And bees being bees, they did what they wanted and laughed at me as well.

I'd heard other beekeepers lament that beekeeping required lots of equipment, but I was in disbee-lief. Surely one extra honey box per hive would be enough; I'd remove it when it was full, extract the honey right away, and immediately get the box back on the hive.

You seasoned beekeepers through laughing about that yet?

That was my plan, but I failed to run it by the bees. And bees being bees, they did what they wanted and laughed at me as well.

The second summer I kept bees was a warm, humid one—great for things that bees love to pollinate, like clover and dandelions. Every neighbor's flower bed had burst into color, and the bees happily visited each blossom.

All sunny day long, day after day after day, the bees returned to the hive overloaded with nectar and pollen. Soon, the bees had filled every cell of the honey box with golden liquid. They wouldn't put a waxy cap on each cell to seal that honey until they had dried it to the right moisture level, or "cured" it.

Unfortunately, the bees weren't making much progress. Granted, it was hard with the humidity so high and every flower beckoning. My plan for a single honey box per hive wasn't working; the bees needed more space to store honey, or they might swarm off and find one. While their making lots and lots of honey was truly super, what was I to do?

So yes, you super by adding a super. Confusing, yes, but much of beekeeping is.

Oh yeah, super.

In my part of the country, a typical hive has two deep boxes, which house the bees, the nursery, and the honey they'll need to survive a typical winter. When it is peak honey-making season, you give the bees additional, shorter boxes. That honey is for humans. As the honey they put in those short boxes is superfluous to the bees, the boxes have earned the name "supers."

In addition to "super" being a noun, it is also a verb. When you put the box on the hive, you super. So yes, you super by adding a super. Confusing, yes, but much of beekeeping is.

The one super per hive plan wasn't working. I obtained more short (also known as easier to lift off when full) boxes to give the bees more room for honey.

The bees continued to be super at producing honey that summer, but not at curing it. Within a few weeks I, and they, had the same lack-of-space problem.

I purchased more supers, and supered again. I'm nearly six feet tall, but this

 © 2014 Charlotte Hubbard | www.hubbardhive.com

made the height of the hives a bit much for even me. I wondered if any lanky NBA players wanted to learn about beekeeping.

My wonderfully productive bees filled up those new supers also. The honey remained uncapped. Buying even more equipment would solve the problem for a few weeks, but I just couldn't keep doing that. Not only was my beekeeping budget low, but come fall, all those boxes would need to come off the hives and be stored somewhere.

I had some deep boxes hanging out, unused. And so I deeped.

The varying heights of these hives underscore how colonies produce differently. The second, third and sixth from the left kept filling up those shorter boxes faster than they could dry the honey. Thus, by the time the hive on the far right needed extra room, I had to use the taller (deep) boxes, usually reserved for bees' honey storage and nursery.

My computer's spell-checker doesn't like the word "supered." It doesn't like "deeped" either. Nor do I. If the bees also filled up those boxes with honey, that'd be a super. But, a deep box, when filled up with honey, weighs nearly 100 pounds. I'm a large, strong farm girl, but lifting 100 pounds off a tall stack while being serenaded by stinging insects wasn't all that fun.

Hmmm. I wondered if any beefy NFL players wanted to learn about beekeeping.

If so, that'd be *super!*

Really?!

Because of beekeeping, I routinely use a bunch of words that I didn't know five years ago, like *supering, brood chamber* and *hot hive*. The latter is a hive that comes out to greet you before you get close, hell-bent on stinging you for no apparent reason.

Because there is such a thing as a *hot hive*, I've also used a bunch of words that would've made my mother wash out my mouth with soap. Beekeeping doesn't cause me to swear—very often. It does cause me to say "Really?!" a great deal though. Yes, really.

For example, there was this situation with a hive going into winter a bit light on stores. I gave them syrup in a feeder placed inside the hive. Every few days I'd refilled that feeder, for over a month. I figured the bees were used to me popping the top by then, but I always suited up, just in case.

On a sunny October day, I wore my half-suit, perfect for a fall day when I'm already in jeans. When I removed the top cover, I found a bone-dry feeder and a lot of eyes staring at me. And by a lot of eyes, I mean probably a quarter million or so. Honeybees have hundreds of single eyes, each with its own lens, and each usually looking in a different direction—except this time the quarter million eyes were all staring at me hungrily. And accusingly.

And undeservingly. "Sure I'm a little late ladies," I muttered. "But there's still goldenrod out there, no need to just hang around the hive hoping I'd show up with lunch."

Was stinging me necessary? Really?!

The bees ignored what I said, and then ignored me as they greedily swarmed the syrup. I gently closed the hive. This was yet another time when I'd worn protective clothing for nothing, but better safe than sorry.

I began walking away. Within seconds I saw my mistake. Well, actually, I felt it. I hadn't checked my legs to verify that they were honeybee-free before I left the apiary. One must've landed on me, and—having felt threatened by my movement—promptly stung me on my "seat."

My first reaction was pain. Even through the jeans, there was no mistaking what that burning spike meant.

My second reaction was "Really??!!" Did she miss the lesson on "Don't bite the hand that feeds you? And don't sting her tail either?"

I've been stung through jeans before. There's the initial sharp pain, but because the stinger can't really embed, it's typically no big deal. This one however was a big deal, for two reasons. First, because I really couldn't believe that a bee would

Really? I'm supposed to put the cover back on without injuring any of you?!

give up her life as I was trying to help save the lives in her hive, and second, because of where she stung me. My tail doesn't need to be any larger.

As I rubbed my quickly swelling backside, the guardian honeybee fell to the ground, her backside beyond repair. Poor dear. Was stinging necessary? Really?!

As examples of some of the many other times I've used that word while working bees:

Really?! You think swarming on Labor Day is a good idea?[3]

Really?! You thought crawling in that little gap by the zipper would end well for either of us?

Really?! You wanted to see my bathroom? How and when did you get in the house?

Really?! You think swarming *again* mid-September is a good idea?

Really?! You thought it'd be fun to ride in the car? With fifteen of your friends?

Really?! You thought four of you chasing my bee-loving niece a quarter of a mile would be good exercise for her?

Really?! You thought I couldn't remove that last super even with 45 pounds of propolis[4] gluing it down?

I suspect bees have used their own version of "Really??!!" regarding us humans, including:

Really?! You can go to the moon but you can't do anything about Varroa?

Really?! You *think* we can't find a way through all that "protective" clothing?

Really?! You think we wanted to swarm again mid-September? We had to because _____. (The bees will have to fill in the blank because I sure as heck have no idea why they swarmed again in September.)

---

3   That's late in the season to get a new colony ready for winter.
4   Propolis is a resinous, very binding mixture bees collect from trees, etc., and used to seal undesired hive spaces.

Plastic bears sporting our unique line of honey bear accessories. It is so hard to get these models to look into the camera at the same time.

Really?! You think putting on a mouse guard after the field mice were already in our hive was helpful?

Really?! You think we enjoy seeing our life's work poured into plastic bears?

Really?! We make honey and we share it. You make mead[5] and you don't. And you wonder why we sting you in the tail?!

OK bees, that last one is an exceptionally good point. Really.

Mouse Guards?

Mouse guards reduce the entrance so that critters seeking a warm home, complete with honey, don't move in as winter approaches. Typically we put on the guards late fall, when the bees' activities have slowed down. The smaller doorway can be disruptive to an active hive.

The timing is tricky. A couple of times I put on guards when winter came too quickly. It was too cold to open the hives and make sure there were no critters inside—and oops, there were.

I discovered the first occurrence one unseasonably warm March day. I had removed the mouse guard to scrape out any dead bees. A very much

While I don't like critters in my hives, I don't wish dying this way on anything. There were about 20 dead bees imbedded in its fur; I suspect it was stung to death while trapped inside the hive.

alive mouse, probably trapped in there the previous fall, came roaring out. If you were anywhere in the USA at the time, you probably heard me scream.

That mouse was lucky that the bees hadn't gotten to it yet. Another time I opened a hive in early spring and found a critter nest, complete with a dead critter in it, stung to death.

---

5   Mead is an alcoholic beverage made from fermented honey.

Swarming

"Swarming" is an incredible event where several thousand bees, perhaps as many as 25,000 of them, maniacally rush out of the hive and swirl off in a buzzing cloud to find a new home. Witnessing such an event was once on my bucket list—I'd heard you could practically feel the gust of air as they swoop off, and that the sound is incredible.

Cross off that item.

A nice swarm. It was a decent size, reachable, and didn't mind have its picture taken.

Seeing bees swarm was astonishing. And awesome. And regretful, because too often the bees I've watched soar off are my own. Yes, there was an incredible rush of air and an almost deafening roar as they swirled by. I could still hear them laughing at me however.

As amazing as it is to witness, we beekeepers *hate* seeing our bees swarm. While there's no way to prevent swarming other than keeping bees in a box, oh wait, we keep bees in a box.

While there's no way to prevent swarming other than keeping bees in a vault, there are certain things a beekeeper can do to discourage it. And often, bees swarm anyway. When that happens, it seems personal.

Another reason we beekeepers take it hard is because, while bees know what's best for bees, swarming puts both those who go and those who stay behind at risk.

A swarm consists of about half the bees of the parent colony. Thus, the bees left behind lose half their workforce and their queen. It'll take a few weeks for a new virgin queen to develop. When she does, she'll have to successfully find and mate with drones (sometimes as many as two dozen of them!) It's a glorious afternoon for her, but she still has to make it home safely without mating with a Ford Explorer or a bird's belly.

Nor did they mind being carried across the yard and placed in a new home.

The thousands of bees who swarmed are also at risk. They have to find a new location and hope that they don't run into a can of bug spray.

Of course, we beekeepers also *love* it when bees swarm, as long as they aren't our bees. Swarming is how bees naturally reproduce. They wouldn't do it if they didn't feel grand about their strength and workforce. And the thrill of pursuing and capturing a swarm is always worthy of a story or six...

 © 2014 Charlotte Hubbard | www.hubbardhive.com

Pants Are Overrated

Fire departments, bee clubs, pest control companies and the like have people to call who will come and capture a fugitive swarm of bees. I'm on a couple of these swarm lists. During swarm season (typically spring), I keep the phone handy, hoping when it rings that the person on the other end wants me to take away a ball of stinging insects. Most beekeepers love to capture swarms, but the timing can be tricky. You have to be ready to drop everything and go after them because a swarm doesn't (usually) stay around long.

I've solved this timing challenge, because over the years, I've figured out when swarms will occur: whenever I'm going out of town.

For example, I travelled out of state in early June. The first swarm call came within minutes of crossing into Indiana. A woman a mere three miles from my house had a basketball-sized swarm of honeybees hanging from a tomato cage, which I also could have if I'd please-please-please take the bees away. She begged me to turn back.

I couldn't, and apologized profusely. I was truly, very, very sorry. I wanted both the bees and the tomato cage.

Upon awakening the next day, 600 miles from home, I checked my phone. Two new messages. Two new swarms. Both allegedly mammoth; both within ten feet of the ground. I like to think that honeybees don't plot ways to mock me, but the

second caller said the swarm cackled and handed him my phone number on a small piece of paper.

We returned home three days later. My phone was oddly silent, much like our spoiled cat who was pouting because we had abandoned him (with a cat sitter nonetheless.)

The next day I awoke to a sunshiny, low humidity, perfect Michigan day, and a phone call. Glory bee! The caller, a spirited, delightful retiree named Jimmy, had a swarm.

Jimmy lived only a mile away. Jimmy said the swarm was half his size and hanging just a few feet off the ground on a tree in his backyard. It seemed too good to be true, and of course—it was.

Of course this was too good to be true.

We were there in less than 20 minutes, but the swarm was not.

"I still hear them though," I said, recognizing an unmistakable buzz in the air. "Mind if we wander around and see if they settled elsewhere?"

"No problem," answered Jimmy. "But before we stroll, there's a few things you need to know about me."

First, Jimmy wanted us to know that he loved the Lord. Second, he felt it important to share that while he'd help us look, he was extremely afraid of bees. Third, Jimmy insisted that we know that he carried at least one gun with him at all times for protection, and had many more hidden about his property.

To prove it, Jimmy pulled a small gun out of his pocket. He pointed it at the trees slowly, the sun flashing off the metal. Jimmy seemed perplexed that his many guns were useless against the invading honeybees.

We wandered with Jimmy about his picturesque backyard, hoping to find the bees on a nearby, low-hanging branch. Rounding a corner, we heard buzzing (and I swear, giggling.) The swarm had settled about 15 feet up.

Marshall, Jimmy and I stared at the nice-sized cluster for several minutes. Marshall and I stared from directly under it; Jimmy peeked from behind a barn door 20 feet away. Staring doesn't do anything to get bees out of a tree, but every beekeeper I've ever seen capture a swarm spends several minutes just bee-holding it.

Our staring also had a purpose. Marshall and I were plotting ways to reach them. We discussed where to precariously place the ladder, which branches we might have to snip, who would do what. Marshall and I both love heights. If Jimmy agreed with our plan, we'd have a coin toss to determine who got to climb the ladder, and who had the boring job of holding it.

Jimmy was very agreeable to our plan. It involved making the stinging insects go away.

As a precaution, I began pulling on my protective coveralls. Marshall, who prefers just a bee jacket, put it on and oops, in our haste, he'd left the house wearing shorts. His long, hairy legs glistened in the sunlight. I offered to dash home and fetch a pair of pants for Marshall. Our home, containing pants, was a mere mile away.

"Don't bother. Pants are overrated," Marshall shrugged and grabbed the pruning shears.

Jimmy, who was hopping up and down from stinging insect anxiety, gasped. "That's just not right!"

 © 2014 Charlotte Hubbard | www.hubbardhive.com

You know what else isn't right? Overanxious guys with guns in their pockets.

Marshall assured Jimmy it'd likely be just fine, explaining the typical demeanor of swarms. Even if they stung his legs though, Marshall said it'd be all right. Marshall has a cranky ankle and knee. He finds stings to them momentarily painful, but long-term quite helpful.

That only increased Jimmy's already extremely high agitation. "You want stings? That's just crazy. Marshall, it would tickle me pink if I could please lend you some pants."

I sort of wanted Marshall to accept the offer... just so I could see 6'1" Marshall in 5'3" Jimmy's pants.

But, Marshall declined. For a few seconds I wondered if Jimmy would grab one of his guns and insist Marshall put on pants.

Marshall started up the ladder. I held the bottom, although trust me—if the ladder started to sway as Marshall brought the swarm down, you couldn't trust my holding it, protective suit or not. Jimmy made a hasty retreat to behind the barn door.

Marshall demonstrates that pants are overrated.

"By the way," whispered Jimmy loudly from his hiding place, "what church do you attend?"

I found that an interesting question at an interesting time. Did he want to be sure that if Marshall tumbled off the ladder he knew who his Maker was? Or that the bees were going to a good Christian home?

Sometimes swarm captures go as planned, and this was one of them. Marshall went up the ladder; the bees on a branch came down with him; none of them even thought about stinging.

We loaded the bees into our car, and Jimmy resumed breathing.

And because no shots were fired, after we drove away, we also resumed breathing.

Up, Up and Away

On a clear, sunny, great-to-be-a-bee Saturday in July, I decided to say hi to my backyard hives. It's part of being a beekeeper, this wanting to check on, send kisses to and spend time with your bees.

Wandering toward the apiary, I heard a lot of buzzing.

The buzzing was steadily increasing. I surveyed the hives; there wasn't enough activity to justify it.

Following the sound to a nearby maple tree, my eyes went up and my jaw dropped down. A swarm was just settling in the top of the towering tree.

If staring at the bees could bring them down, they'd be in a hive.

I exaggerate. The swaying cluster of bees was not at the top of the tree, but rather only about 60 feet up. It might as well have been on the moon.

I glared at my bees. These were first-year hives. Don't the bees read the books that say they don't typically swarm the first year?!

And doggone it, it was July. Swarms in July aren't supposed to be worth the effort to capture them. What's that old expression? Swarm in May, worth a load of hay; June, silver spoon; July, not worth a fly? Painful sigh? Poke a stick in the beekeeper's eye?

Not this beekeeper's eye! I have ladders, ropes, life insurance and no fear of heights. My only dependents are a high-maintenance dog and a rotund cat who rarely leaves the couch. If the worst happened as I attempted to retrieve the bees who I paid $100 for only a few months earlier, there'd be enough money to get the dog some therapy and hire a forklift to move the hefty cat to my daughter's house. What was stopping me from risking life and limb?

Upon further examination, a lot. The swarm had settled near the end of a slender limb, with no nearby limbs to support my weight. Even if I gave up chocolate immediately, an extreme action I *might* consider doing for bees, it'd take weeks of dieting before I could safely venture out on that limb. They'd have flown off by then.

 © 2014 Charlotte Hubbard | www.hubbardhive.com

After my husband passed away, several neighbors had said "If you ever need anything, just call."

So I did.

Neighbor Dr. Pete arrived first, much to my relief. Dr. Pete isn't a medical doctor—that would be handy if I fell out of the tree—but he has an engineering PhD. Maybe, with ladders and pulleys and ropes, he could figure out a way to get my humming escapees to the ground.

Soon neighbor Paul arrived, lured by the opportunity to use his chain saw.

While Paul and Pete conferred; I continued to give my bees dirty looks. Didn't they know their chances of making it out in the big world were not that great? Why wouldn't they listen to me, the real queen bee, and stay? Didn't they know I had things to do other than stare up at the tree and wonder what I did wrong?! Did they have something against me personally?

More neighbors swarmed into my backyard, bringing dogs, little kids, and unbridled curiosity. If staring at the bees could bring them down, they'd be in a hive.

After studying the situation, and consuming the two complimentary beers I handed him, Dr. Pete concluded there was no safe way to retrieve the traitors.

The gathered throng of neighbors saluted Dr. Pete's analysis, and everyone went home. Except, of course, the bees. They continued to look down upon me and their old home.

When something goes awry, my first call is usually to neighbor Wayne. Wayne has a high school diploma and a PhD in practical knowledge, which is why he is my go-to guy. He'd been my first call that Saturday. I'd left a message about the bees because he wasn't home.

Wayne returned my call the next morning. I explained that some folks with substantial educational credentials had suggested that we couldn't get the swarm out of the tree.

The gauntlet was thrown. Within the hour Wayne was in my backyard with saws, ropes, and an attitude.

We removed all limbs below the still sleepy swarm; the bees seemingly didn't care.

We set out a dark, inviting hive with a luring scent on a white bed sheet beneath the swarm[1]. The bees seemingly didn't care.

The plan was to cut the limb that held the swarm, such that it would fall to the ground. Confused and exposed, the bees would hopefully scamper into the hive. They might care about that part.

We double-checked our protective gear, and talked through the plan a final time. Please note that the bees WERE part of this discussion.

Please also note that bees can't hear.

Toward the end of this discussion, based on some unknown signal, the ball of bees began to loosen. Within seconds they were a cloud. Within a minute, the bees had swirled away over the house. Hmmm. I guess they did care.

I tried to find the silver lining in the cloud of bees that had disappeared into the sky. Looking on the bright side, a swarm typically means a strong colony, so I must've had one, not that I had much to do with that.

It was my loss for sure, but a gain for bee biological diversity in southwest Michigan. They'd find different colonies with whom to mate.

The event also reminded me that I live next to some great neighbors.

If only I also still lived next to those honeybees.

---

1   The theory is that the bees don't like being exposed and hanging out in such strong light, so they'll move to the dark hole, especially if it smells like a queen bee.

 © 2014 Charlotte Hubbard | www.hubbardhive.com

Swarming to the Party

The prelude to any outdoor event—weddings, parades, graduation parties—is a season of worry. Will it be too warm? Is there enough food? What if it storms? What if everyone comes at once? Or no one comes?

Beekeeper Dov and new graduate Sarah.

Wally's family worried about those things for daughter Sarah's high school graduation party. And as is so often true in life, all that worry was for naught. While the day was perhaps a bit warm, the food was fabulous and guests came and went over time, allowing for everyone to relax in the shade in the beautiful backyard.

A few uninvited guests showed up. It happens—perhaps some high school friends brought along some other friends. No big deal. There were certainly enough barbecue meatballs.

And then a few more uninvited guests show up. They seemed to find each other as if their appearance was all part of some unspoken plan to crash the party. It was all a bit annoying, really. Showing up uninvited is one thing, but these guests huddled together in an antisocial cluster and couldn't even be bothered to mingle with the other guests. *Oh well, what are you going to do?* the party-goers decided.

But then even more uninvited guests showed up.

The other attendees were distracted by this growing number of anti-socialites. They couldn't help but notice that their behavior and demeanor were different, that they didn't bother to even say hello to Sarah, that they clustered on the side away from most people, that they all had stingers.

My brother-in-law Jim was invited to Sarah's graduation party. Jim was sipping an icy beverage and making small talk when he, like so many others, noticed the uninvited guests gathering on a limb over a picnic table. He immediately called me on the phone.

"On the phone," he said, "What are you doing RIGHT NOW?"

I explained that I'd just come in from working hives thirty minutes away. I'd unloaded all our bee equipment from the vehicle, and was very hot, very sweaty and very hungry.

"Well," he explained, "I'm at a graduation party with a swarm of bees. You interested? There's really good meatballs too."

Free bees? Absolutely. And meatballs? Bonus! We reloaded equipment and headed out.

If I'd understood prior to meeting him what a great sense of humor that Sarah's father Wally had, my beekeeping buddies and I would've fully suited up and "ghostbusted" our way into the party. But, not knowing if we'd freak out folks, we first subtly slipped in to check out the swarm. We even grabbed lemonade and meatballs (and brownies and chips and some more meatballs) so it looked like we were real guests.

I stood there in my bee suit with a meatball in my mouth.

Nonchalantly we made our way to the bees. It wasn't difficult. The other guests were giving them plenty of space.

It was a small swarm, conveniently reachable with a small step ladder. The grad party was winding down. Because the bees showed no sign of leaving, and many of the guests had already gone, we decided to capture them.

We brought in a box and stepladder. We suited up—tucking pants into socks, checking that our gloves were snug, zipping our hoods, all with a flourish. Thinking about Facebook and the graduation scrapbook, Wally posed us for pictures with guest-of-honor Sarah, who declined our invitation to wear the extra bee suit and help.

We brushed the bees off the limb and they largely fell into the box with a swoosh and a splat. Several dozen bees circled the spot on the limb where the small swarm had initially gathered. I explained to Wally that we'd probably just let them, well, be. If we opened the box to sweep them in, we'd let an equal number out. But we'd hang out for a while to make sure there weren't more than a few dozen resettling on the limb (and because the cake was really good).

Besides, what always happens when folks learn you're a beekeeper was happening: people were swarming us with questions. As I stood there in my bee suit with a meatball in my mouth, a grinning guest came up to me.

"Be straight with me," he gestured with his carrot stick. "Everything Wally does is over-the-top, a bit beyond the usual. Did he hire you guys to do this? Because people will be talking about the graduation party with the bees all summer."

He was joking—I think.

I explained that we weren't hired. We were certainly willing to show up in bee suits at social events—for a fee of course. But, it is hard to hire bees who will swarm to the specified location at the right time. Bees are well-known for swarming to wherever they want, at the wrong time.

After about 15 minutes (or, if you're counting calories, after about 3,000 more), we left with our new bees and a couple of cookies. Within an hour, they were installed at my apiary. The bees, not the cookies, although those were also "installed."

We named the hive Sarah.

Two months later, the Sarah hive had doubled in size, and seems well on its way to building up for the winter.

We hope its future is as bright as the young lady's whose party they crashed.

Why Do Bees Swarm?

On a dreary weekday in April, a weekday that had me asking "is spring ever going to come to Michigan?" I booked a last-minute, four-days-away vacation to Florida. I'd had it with the snow, the cold, the grey clouds.

That weekend, Michigan weather being Michigan weather, the skies cleared and the sun came out. As my flight was cleared for take-off, eight colonies of bees in my area also took off.

Upon landing in Florida—only hours later!—I turned on my cell phone. There were *eight* frantic voice mails from folks who had clusters of bees hanging on swing sets, bushes, shrubs, and a basketball hoop. Could I please come take them away?

Eight. Yes, eight, doggone it! Eight families' nightmares and the stuff of my dreams. Eight free, happy colonies that would've nicely expanded my apiary! Eight!! Sure, I already have plenty of colonies. But bees, like money and chocolate, well, you can never have enough.

I returned each call from the frantic folks who had found me on a swarm list. I explained that I was unavailable that weekend, and encouraged them to contact another beekeeper. If they couldn't get hold of another beekeeper, I'd handle the swarm upon my return, if it was still there.

Upon returning home, I learned that all eight swarms had indeed moved on. I focused on working my own bees, and had a grand time doing so. The next time I'd be away from the apiary was late August, for a long-planned family vacation.

The honey of a summer flew by. I spent countless hours in the apiary, trying to keep the bees happy as best I knew how. As August came to a close, we packed for vacation and did final checks of the hives before leaving for the north woods of Canada. We thought we left the bees with everything they needed to be content and stay home... and then we somewhat ironically left home. I hoped we weren't setting a bad example.

Our vacation took us far away from everything, including cell phone service. A week later, when we returned to civilization and a phone signal, there were five messages on my phone. Once again, while I was on vacation, bees had swarmed.

It was late August. As I listened to the folks begging me to make the scary stinging insects go away, I couldn't help but think of that oft-quoted poem:

 © 2014 Charlotte Hubbard | www.hubbardhive.com

A swarm in May is worth a load of hay;
A swarm in June is worth a silver spoon;
A swarm in July, let her fly.

The poem stops abruptly without suggesting the value of a swarm in August. That's probably because a swarm in August isn't worth much—not enough time for the colony to build up for winter survival or produce any honey for humans.

Of course, it might also be because nothing easily rhymes with "August."

I listened to the phone messages again. One guy called twice—first to let me know he had a swarm, and then again to let me know it had happily flown away. A near-hysterical woman named Diane had called three times, begging me to please come and make those bees go.

Diane's calls had been left on Tuesday, Wednesday and Thursday. It was now Saturday; I wouldn't be home until Sunday. What were the chances of the bees still being there? About zero.

With a day's travel back home ahead of us, I called Diane to explain why I hadn't responded, and to thank her for trying to help the honeybees that had surely moved on by now. I explained that most bees only stay a day or two when swarming, and—

Judging by the number of empty cans at their feet, the adults had been there longer than the bees had been.

Diane interrupted to tell me that the bees had moved sure enough, but only to a different place in the yard. "And their ball is getting bigger, every day!" she yowled. "When can you get here?! I called around; no one wants these bees!"

It'd be Sunday before I could get there—at the earliest, I explained, and emphasized that the swarm would probably be gone by then. And then, for one of the few times in my life, I was glad vacation was over. Sure, I was headed home to a pile of bills, an overgrown lawn and a mountain of laundry, but also, potentially—free bees!

My wake-up call Sunday was from, you guessed it. The swarm was still very much there; Diane still very much frantic. We unloaded the vacation luggage, loaded bee capturing equipment, and headed out.

En route, I thought about why a swarm on Day 6 of moving on hadn't moved far.

Perhaps, having finally left their hive after weeks of planning, they glanced at the calendar and realized it said "August," not "April." A few trees sported fall colors at their edges. I'll bet the old hive was starting to look really good again.

With Diane's address in my GPS, I navigated through a residential area to a dead-end street. Approaching its end, I speculated which of the two remaining homes was likely Diane's. I'll describe them. See if you can guess...

The first house was a quiet one-story home with only a few trees, all of them small.

The second home, surrounded by towering walnut trees, was adjacent to a public school, had three large, loud, barking dogs in a large cage, three small, loud, bouncing children in a trampoline cage, an uncountable number of kids riding bikes and Barbie Doll cars and plastic horses in circles, and nearly a dozen adults staked out in lawn chairs. Judging by the number of empty cans at their feet, the adults had been there longer than the bees had been.

Yep, you guessed correctly. And now, I understood why the bees had stayed. They were enjoying the three-ring circus.

"Are you the bee person?" The calm, grey-haired woman rising out of her lawn chair offered me her hand, but not a drink.

I confirmed I was, and asked if she was Diane. She seemed so unruffled.

"Yes I am," she answered. "And you're too late. The bees left about twenty minutes ago."

Argh.

But, it was all for the best. Getting a swarm of bees out of a tree with a swarm of children, pets and plastic cars below probably wouldn't have gone that well.

While I didn't get the benefit of free bees, like most swarm calls, I was rewarded by meeting some great people who were trying to do the right thing.

I was also rewarded by learning an update for that old poem: "For a swarm in the month of eight, chances are, you're too late."

 © 2014 Charlotte Hubbard | www.hubbardhive.com

Splitting to Prevent Swarming

Until May, high school cheer leading was about the last time I did splits, and high school was—well—a woman isn't supposed to reveal her true age. When I was in high school though, dirt had just recently been invented, and the Devil was still designing the Varroa mite [2].

But now, billions of years after high school, I find myself again doing splits—splits of several hives.

When you have a colony strong enough to split into two colonies, well glory bee! It's a wonderful beekeeping milestone.

I achieved such a milestone my fourth year of keeping bees. And by March of 2013, in a first for me, not only had all hives survived the winter, but most of them were *thriving*. Golly, I must be a stellar beekeeper.

As I throw out my shoulder patting myself on my back, I must also confess that golly, I have no idea how all my hives managed to overwinter. I believe a lot of luck was involved—a lot of luck and not too many of those dang Varroa mites.

Stepson Lucas has another method of doing splits involving bees.

When a colony emerges strong in the spring, beekeepers will often separate it into two colonies, called making a split. The beekeeper gains a hive that way, and it breaks up the breeding cycle of that nasty, prolific mite. Another advantage of doing a split is that it can diminish the bees' urge to swarm, as it is never desirable to see half your bees fly off.

One method of splitting a hive is called a walk-away split. I read extensively about it, and decided to follow that method, but also to integrate a unique spin on it, call it the "Charlotte Twist."

---

2   The Varroa mite, aptly name *Varroa destructor*, is an external, parasitic mite that weakens bees by attaching to them and sucking their bodily fluids. When these mites were discovered in the U.S. in the late 1980s, they had wreaked havoc on honeybee survival, and continue to do so.

In a true walk-away split, you place the required amount of eggs, brood and helper bees in a hive, and walk away. The bees will figure out fairly quickly that they don't have a queen, and begin the delicate process of making one by feeding royal jelly to an egg. The books say to leave them, well, bee for a few weeks to not interrupt their critical efforts.

With the Charlotte-twist, you place the same resources in a hive and walk away—until the next day. That day (and the next day and the next day and next and next) you hover around the split, clutching your hive tool behind your back, and repeatedly reminding yourself that it's too early to open the hive and that you need to just walk away and let them bee, that disturbing them could ruin everything.

Ignore this temptation to open and check it for as many days as you possibly can. Bite down on your hive tool if need be.

In an amazing display of self-restraint, I held off checking on my split until curiosity devoured me the tenth day. I recommend following the rules, but boy-oh-boy, this time I was glad I broke them. One of the hives had nothing but frames of drone, or boy, brood. Hard for them to make a girl bee from thousands of boy eggs.

I loved making splits—even if, like that hive, they're not successful. It needs to be done in the spring, so it's a great excuse to avoid spring cleaning. And, setting the stage for bees to work their magic is addictive. When one split proved successful, well, I felt like I'd laid the new queen's thousands of eggs myself.

I can no longer do splits of the cheer leading kind, but some of that experience has come back to me: Good Job, Bees! Go Team Go!

Just Split, Before They Split

Experienced beekeepers recommend splitting a strong hive to diminish the bees' inclination to swarm. But, figuring out when to do so is a challenge.

If you split it too early in the season, we're cautioned, the queen may not successfully mate, the developing bees may be chilled by weather variations, and you may be cursed for a lifetime such that your cherry pies will forever overflow while baking.

If you split too late in the season and fail to prevent swarming, well, a big ball of your bees will mock you from the top of a maple.

Thus, the easy answer to when you should split a hive is *before they swarm.*

Of course, the hard question is figuring out about when they're going to swarm.

Swarming is often a surprise to beekeepers, but never to bees. It takes them a few weeks to get organized and prepared, and there are a few telltale signs if you are in the hive and able to spot them.

... you may be cursed for a lifetime such that your cherry pies will forever overflow while baking.

Unfortunately, when you live in a place with weather extremes like Michigan, you can't easily check inside the hive because it snows in the morning and then hits 90 degrees in the afternoon. Before you get your mittens off and your bee veil on to peer into a hive, the bees will have swarmed to the top of a newly leafed maple.

When a colony of bees emerges strong from the winter in our bee yards, we split them to discourage the swarming instinct.

But as a back-up measure, there's a set of swarming rules posted in the apiary.

They include:

Rule #1:
NO SWARMING!

But, if you truly must:

- Refer to Rule #1
- And if you insist, then please—48 hours notice
- Swarm only to locations easily visible and accessible to me
- Temperature and humidity must both be well below 90°
- No holiday swarming
- Settle only on small branches no more than five feet off the ground, please pretty please on *my* property
- Swarm only when I see you, and when my afternoon is free

Thank you in advance for your cooperation.

I post this for my bees every year. Every year though, at least a hive or two swarms right past the rules.

I hope that, by doing splits each year, that'll be the year it doesn't happen.

While I stand optimistic, I'm haunted by history. Beckoning branches of the tall backyard maple also stand ready.

Stars, Stripes and Bees

I celebrated our country's birthday by packing almost every piece of bee equipment we own into the SUV and heading to our out-apiary for a full day of working bees. Hubby headed to work also, but he wouldn't be having nearly as much fun. Of course, his job has the benefits of a weekly paycheck and no stings. Some you win, some you lose.

Since getting remarried I've rarely worked bees alone. Honestly, I was looking forward to a leisurely day with just us girls, and an occasional drone of the insect variety. And if the day went too leisurely, well, Hubby could join us after work. I'd packed his protective suit just in case.

Those words are a hive tool through the heart of any beekeeper.

Upon arriving at the out-apiary, a good half hour away, I lit the smoker... a couple of times. I can work bees all by myself, that's no problem. The troubling part for me is lighting the smoker such that it keeps going. My drone of the human variety typically handles that. Oh well. The day was young, and there were over 200 matches in the box. Based on my ability to keep a smoker burning that wasn't enough, but they'd get me through most of the day.

I had just zipped the final closure on my suit when my cell phone rang. As I wasn't yet abuzz in tens of thousands of bees, I answered it.

The caller was a neighbor who lived a half-dozen houses from me. There was a swarm of bees on her ornamental apple tree, and she wanted them gone. Could I help with that?

I assured her that I most certainly could, but it would be a few hours.

"I'll just go ahead and kill them then," her voice was laced with hysteria. "There are too many kids running around here to risk it, and I want to work outside."

"Kill them?!" Those words are a hive tool through the heart of any beekeeper.

Her statement, and knowing the bit about her that I did, made me realize that quick action was necessary. I could explain until I was blue in the face that swarming bees are usually at their most docile. I could suggest parking a few vehicles near the tree to deter kids from running near it. But, like so many people, she didn't understand honeybees, she'd had bad experiences with stinging insects, and wouldn't have heard a word I said. She wanted these honeybees "out of her hair" to make sure they never got into it. Time was critical.

Chances are any swarm north of Arkansas is from one of my hives.

I want to save all bees. I especially wanted to save those bees, because, as the only beekeeper in our subdivision, chances are that swarm came from one of my hives. Of course, my bees have swarmed so much over the years that chances are any swarm north of Arkansas is from one of my hives.

Unfortunately, I needed to expand the hives in my out-apiary or they might feel over crowded and also swarm. That would take at least an hour... and another half hour back home. I called my husband at work.

"At work," I said, explaining the situation. "Any chance you could take an early lunch?"

Hubby loves a swarm as much as I do, but reminded me that he'd ridden his bike the nine miles to work on this perfect summer day. He would see what he could do about the swarm if he could find someone to lend him a vehicle. I said it'd need to be a really fast one. Time was ticking for those bees.

A vehicle wasn't the only thing Hubby was going to need. I had all of our bee equipment in mine—like our swarm trap and queen lure, our sugar-syrup spray bottle, the bee brush, and Hubby's suit. He said he'd calm the neighbor and assess the situation, but I should hurry and zip home with the equipment.

I calmly but quickly worked in the out-apiary. Many bees buzzed before my phone did, but the long-awaited call finally came.

"Is the swarm still there? Is it big?" I asked. "Shall I head that way?"

Hubby reported that the bees were still there, all 78 or maybe 79 of them.

Uh-oh. Any time you can practically count how many bees are in a swarm, it isn't a lot of bees.

I puffed the smoker a few times to make sure it was still going, as disappointed as Hubby was.

"I found an old veil at home and just went ahead and got them," he explained. "One got me back. I didn't realize she was under my arm."

Ouch, and I wasn't even the one stung. I refrained from saying that getting stung there must've been the pits.

"They're in a large shoebox. Good looking queen. When you get home we need to get them into one of the small hives you took with you."

"By the way," Hubby continued. "I don't think they are our bees. They're smaller and darker than anything we have."

This brought a smile to my face. Genetic diversity is a wonderful thing.

A small swarm, but as it contained a queen, we could help it thrive, and thus the smile on beekeeper Marshall's face.

With a renewed spring in my step, I finished up the work that had to be done at the out-apiary, and headed home.

Life was good. Ahead of me were new bees who would soon have a pretty orange hive of their own. The thriving bees at the out-apiary were miles behind me. And immediately behind me, in the back seat of the SUV, was a smoker making up for years of being difficult, and now bellowing clouds of sage-scented smoke.

As I pulled off the road to again extinguish the smoker, I saw a bright side to this small dilemma. Granted, it was becoming harder to see anything, but for the first time in five years, I had managed to get a smoker going quite well.

I coughed and waited for the vehicle to clear, and I couldn't help but smile. At that moment, life was a party, part of a big birthday party for the USA. God bless America, and my new bees, and our neighbor for letting us do the right thing.

And I guess even my smoker.

Bee Careful What You Wish For

On Labor Day weekend, I labored.

It was a labor of love though, because it was with my bees. Even though it was swimsuit weather, I took advantage of the long weekend to begin fall preparations. In the Midwest, sometimes we go from swimsuits to snowsuits in just days.

The hive-checking exercise (and wow, lifting heavy honey-filled boxes is exercise!) reinforced why you should have more than one hive. Bees rarely perform like the books describe. When you have multiple hives you'll see differences. Figuring out why makes you a better beekeeper.

Of course, it takes a lot to figure out bees. I'll let you know if I ever get there.

I'm blessed to have multiple hives, and bee-wildered by how much they vary in disposition and production. For example, 2012's honey of a hive was a first-year colony, located under a towering pine. Those golden darlings delightfully yielded their fourth (!!) box of honey for us by Labor Day. They were named the "Power Hive."

Located just a few feet from these wonderful overachievers is another first-year hive that concerned me all summer. Opening them on Labor Day proved that my suspicions were correct. The bees were wearing silly hats and partying, seemingly unconcerned about the approaching winter. Pesky, no-good wax moths, whom a stronger, work-focused colony would've chased off, were lurking in the corners, selling counterfeit watches.

This hive had been named the "Party Hive" earlier in the season. Party over, Ladies. They had insufficient stores to make it through the winter. Something drastic had to be done.

Because they seem to enjoy leisure activities, I gave the Party Hive a couple of sheets of newspaper to read. I first cut thin slits in the newspaper and placed it over a strong hive, and then put the Party Hive atop the newspaper. If this sounds a lot like the newspaper method for combining two hives into one, you're right.

But, the bees of Party Hive, being bees that had been dancing atop honeycomb all summer, seemed unconcerned about being relocated to a hive buzzing with a mighty work ethic. Sure, for a few hours the residents of the former Party Hive did seem a bit disoriented, but that's partly because they were missing

 © 2014 Charlotte Hubbard | www.hubbardhive.com

their queen, who was smashed. And by "smashed," well, that's what I mean[3].

Combining a weak hive with a strong one left me with some extra, now vacant equipment. Thinking about the many swarm retrieval calls I've historically received in the fall, I said to myself, "Self, wouldn't it be great to have a swarm now?"

There's a reason they say "be careful what you wish for." (If this were an audio book, there'd be spooky music playing now.)

That day I continued my bee work, removing the excess honey and extracting it.

Two days later I put the extracted frames back on various hives. Extraction doesn't remove all the honey, and you want the frames "dry" so they don't mold or attract pests over the winter. Temporarily returning those frames to the hives gives the bees a little snack—they lick dry the honeycomb.

When I opened Power Hive's lid, surprisingly, the bees hardly paid attention to me. There were lots of them gathered at the top of the hive though—far more than I expected to see. What a truly powerful hive.

I glanced down at their bottom entrance—no bees there. This was odd. Usually you'd see some foragers coming and going, or at least some guard bees watching. Nothing.

And then, something. A few bees crawled out the front door to the landing board and took off, and then a few more, and then the dam broke. In less than a minute, an amber-brown torrent of insects gushed from the mouth of the hive, and swirled about and filled the air with buzzing bodies. I could've thrown myself across the hive door but they would've just pushed me aside. I was in the middle of a swarm and there was nothing I could do except watch in awe at the thousands and thousands of insects pouring out. It was very amazing, but doggone it! While I'd wanted to capture a swarm, I didn't want it from one of my hives!

I looked at that abnormal number of bees still hanging out at the top of the hive. They looked back at me a bit sheepishly. A bunch of them rushed to hide a map of the local area. Experts say if you look closely enough, you can find signs of pending swarm activity. They're correct. And if I find whoever gave those bees a map...

After I closed up the hive, I began looking for where the swarm may have settled. I first looked at the top of the tallest nearby tree. Sure enough. And of course they were giggling.

---

3   When you combine two hives, there can only be one queen. Killing the less-desired queen, instead of leaving them to duke it out and possibly kill each other, is an approach many beekeepers take.

I glared at them. They didn't care.

I shouted that it was September! According to the old adage, a swarm in September is worth... nothing! That's because it's nearly impossible to survive when you're starting over in September. What were they thinking?! What was their goal?! (Besides making a fool out of this beekeeper.)

I've heard of various ways to get a swarm out of a tree top. One method involves using a power washer to blast them down. I've got a power washer and the scars to prove that I don't know how to use it safely—but that's a future book, perhaps titled "My Top 10 Stupid Things I've Done Involving Bees."

This was a futile attempt to blast a different swarm out of the top of the tree. The power washer wasn't powerful enough, although Marshall got a nice shower. Those trees have held many a swarm over the past few years. Maybe I should replace them with all dwarf trees.

I quickly dismissed that power washer approach. I knew from experience that its stream wasn't strong enough to reach and knock out the swarm, although I knew from experience that it was powerful enough to slice gashes into my legs.

Another method for capturing a swarm atop a tree involves shooting an arrow with an attached string over a bough near the swarm. Assuming the arrow falls to earth, you hook a queen-scented frame to the other end of the string, and raise it to the bees. According to the books, (which I'm not sure any bee has ever read), the bees will move to that frame. When they do, you simply lower the frame and bees, and pop them back into a hive, where they'll live happily ever after.

I ruled out that option as it would take waaaaay too long. I'm in my early 50s, and still can't sink a paper wad into a trash can from a mere three feet away. I'm willing to practice, but in the decade it'll take me to learn to accurately use a bow and arrow, I suspect the swarm will have moved elsewhere. I also don't believe in "happily ever after," or bees would still be in the Power Hive.

I glared again at the swarm, but they didn't even see me. When you're 70 feet in the air, there's probably more interesting things to look at than an irate beekeeper.

I wondered what other folks do when they have a swarm in their backyard. Oh yeah, they call folks on the swarm list, like me.

It was a long shot, but I sprinkled lemongrass[4] oil in a vacant hive sitting on a wall at the side of my yard. Hopefully the bees would check it out, and move in. I promised them all sorts of assistance if they did—like sugar syrup and high-speed internet. I also wandered back and forth under the tree talking to them and pointing to the bait hive, mentioning what an ideal location it was, and how pretty it was.

They didn't care.

Needing to think some more, I went indoors and began taking off my protective suit, all the while wishing that half the occupants of my most productive hive weren't clustered at the top of a tree.

I really must be more careful about what I wish for. When I went outside 15 minutes later to glare at them some more, they weren't clustered at the top of a tree any longer, they'd already taken off.

Somewhere in the area is half of a really powerful colony. Good luck to you, bees.

---

4   Lemongrass oil emits about the same scent as a queen bee. It is often successfully used to lure bees, for whom scent is a major communication method.

Photo Story of a Swarming Event

1. On one swarm call, we were delighted to find a nice-sized swarm, reachable with a stool. We cut the limb and carried them to an awaiting hive...

2. ... which they poured out of minutes after we closed it up. (We likely hadn't captured the queen.) While only about half the population of the original hive, it was still a brown river of insects hurling out.

3. And then the air looked like this!

4. The swarm resettled into two, a bit higher up the same tree. The second capture required a ladder, but we got them—and they stayed.

 © 2014 Charlotte Hubbard | www.hubbardhive.com

Swarming Summary

Here are some other interesting points about this awesome, natural event called swarming.

After her initial mating flights, the Queen Bee typically becomes too robust to fly. Thus, when the colony is preparing to swarm, they chase her around the hive for a few days to thin her down, and stop feeding her.

When a colony swarms, they typically settle fairly close to where they started, and will hang on that shrub, lawn chair or tractor tire for a day or two while they determine their new address.

When a swarm lands, they're a massive, writhing, shifting cluster of bees, a tangled mass of wings and legs and antenna that sways together through the wind and usually even your cutting off the branch and carrying it. The first law of swarm capture says that when you see a swarm, you must first stand there for a while and say "Oh wow." It's a really easy rule to follow.

The bees in a swarm innately know what to do. Some of them are scouting for their new home; others are pampering the queen; still others are conserving energy for the massive upcoming need to build new honeycomb. It's an impressive, well-oiled machine. Others are assigned the task of waving at stunned humans.

I love swarms, yes, even when they are my bees.

While there are a few things beekeepers can do to try and prevent swarming, no method is guaranteed. But we try, nonetheless. It gives bees something to laugh at.

Bee-ing in Their Presence

Honeybees are responsible
for apple pie, blueberry yogurt and daisies.

They're also responsible for my car seats being sticky
March through November when my car is a
bee-mobile, and my kitchen (and cat)
being sticky whenever it is extraction time.

Melvin gets real annoyed licking honey out of his luxurious fur.
And when I made him wear a silly bee hat

Honeybees have led me to make hundreds of new friends
throughout the world—interesting, introspective people.
I also count these insects as friends. They've caressed and
refreshed my soul, and challenged, educated, stung me, and
laughed at and with me. My glimpses into their enchanting
world have left me humbled and in awe.

Thanks, bees, for allowing me to bee in your presence.

Thunder? I Won't Use the Metal Stepladder...

My nephew Chad recently graduated from the University of Michigan.

I mention U of M because approximately 67% of my children attended this "Harvard of the Midwest." Having written lots of checks for lots of dollars to this university, I try to promote it whenever possible.

Chad's life at the U of M was worlds away from my world of beekeeping. A devoted student, I suspect when Chad heard "bee," he thought about a grade he doesn't want to receive. When he heard "honey," he thought of the cute coed in accounting. Hearing those two words together? Probably didn't happen much in that world of lectures, exams, football, and adult beverages which I'm sure he didn't consume until he was legal.

Nonetheless, one summer day of his collegiate life, Chad helped me work bees on Dad's farm. I think it was because Chad was a bit bored during the visit, but I pretended it was because he wanted to spend quality time with his favorite aunt.

Chad was an excellent rookie beekeeper because he took direction well and didn't freak out. Bonus—he could lift heavy boxes effortlessly. God bless that young, strong back.

After the first hive or two, Chad expressed more than just a "helping Favorite Aunt Charlotte" interest in beekeeping. Much to my delight, he asked great questions, and spotted queens faster than I could. He could even spot eggs, and I haven't seen eggs since I turned 50. For the last few years I thought perhaps queens stopped laying eggs, going instead direct to larvae. But I see now (except for anything close up) that my eyes aren't what they used to be.

Those nearly translucent cylinders, more apparent in the second and third cells of the top row; the first, second and fourth of the second row; and the middle cells of the third row are honeybee eggs. This photo is highly magnified, and courtesy of Dan K.

After our sweaty hours in bee suits, my first goal was to find an adult beverage. Chad's first goal was to post about our adventure on Facebook.

Upon seeing the post, a high school buddy contacted him. Though he and Chad hadn't talked for a couple of years, the young man was so excited that he called

 © 2014 Charlotte Hubbard | www.hubbardhive.com

Chad to discuss a swarm he'd just captured.

"I just can't believe how pumped he was," Chad later shared with me. "He just went on and on about capturing that swarm and bees in general. He has ten hives, and wants to double that."

> Yep, Bee Disease. It's this SUPER-contagious disease you can get—even if you've only been exposed to a hive or two.

I nodded understandably. Way too understandably. "Your buddy has Bee Disease," I stated.

Chad looked at me with alarm.

"Yep, Bee Disease. It's this SUPER-contagious disease you can get—even if you've only been exposed to a hive or two."

Chad asked about the symptoms. I caught Bee Disease the summer of 2008 and haven't shaken it yet, so I'm quite familiar with many of the symptoms, and how the infection progresses.

Bee Disease bee-gins with a longing to "check" your bees even though you may have just checked them, say, 30 minutes ago. I say "check" because that's what you tell your spouse you are going to do. "Checking" makes it sound like something that needs to occur, rather than the irrepressible urge to just go watch bees.

"Checking" your bees too often, like ten times in the same day, would make your family suspicious that you're obsessed with an insect. So, when you have Bee Disease, you get another hive or two (or nine), and justify your need to just hang out with bees by saying you have to go "check" them again because with so many hives, you couldn't visit them all the first time. (Or the second time. Or the third.)

Another symptom of Bee Disease is mental impairment. Examples include:

- You wander down to the apiary to check on the bees for 15 minutes, you swear it was only 15 minutes, but you were gone for so long that your kids grew up.

- You mow around dandelions in your once "weed"-free yard because your new best friends enjoy them so. If a bee-friendly plant sprouts in a crack in your driveway, you water and fertilize it.

- During a raging thunderstorm, you hear about a swarm of bees atop a towering church steeple, and think "Hey, where's my stepladder? I can save those bees." For safety's sake, you ponder using the *wooden* stepladder.

Occasionally, there are physical symptoms of having Bee Disease, like that ache in your lower back from lifting hive boxes, and occasionally, a hard, itchy swollen area where you've taken a sting (or three).

"Whew," Chad sighed. "For a minute you had me worried. I thought this Bee Disease was a real thing."

Oh dear nephew, it is a very real thing. But because Chad is only around his favorite aunt a few times during the year, he isn't impacted by the toll my Bee Disease takes on closer friends and family. They're victim to sticky doorknobs, counters, and faucets during honey extraction. They open the freezer for ice cream, and instead find a frame of honey with frozen wax moths on it. They wash the car only to find it speckled minutes later. They have to park the car on the side of the drive because the garage is full of bee equipment, or because you don't want them to run over the dandelions thriving in the ever-expanding driveway cracks. Fortunately much of their anxiety and frustration can be soothed by handing them a biscuit dripping with honey.

This is the windshield of my car one early spring day, after I parked near hives.
Those brown dots are from bees flying and relieving themselves. The car was covered with such spots.
I was delighted; bees flying in the spring make a beekeeper's heart soar.

As for the person who has Bee Disease—is there anything they can do?

Yes, enjoy it. And use the wooden ladders during thunderstorms.

 © 2014 Charlotte Hubbard | www.hubbardhive.com

Where Some of the Hours Go

Watching a hive on a warm, sunny day is like observing takeoffs and landings at the airport. But probably safer, as long as you don't become something causing a bee's flight delay.

People new to beekeeping are often surprised by the time it takes.

Yes, the initial learning curve is steep, and a new-bee will naturally be slower at working a hive or lighting a smoker. Nonetheless, beekeeping does surprisingly require a lot of time, although it is important to distinguish between the time necessary and the time given oh-so-willingly.

I've sat many hours by the side of the hive, watching bees come and go. As long as you're off to the side, they generally don't seem to mind. It is mesmerizing and meditative.

I shared this photo with a friend, who commented, "Cool, those bees seem happy!"

I think they were. I know I was.

Bee Disease Flare-Up

According to the news, mid-January found most of the country with the flu. Hundreds of thousands of Americans were feeling crummy with aches, chills, coughs, fevers and more.

Knock on wood, I didn't suffer from the flu that weekend. I did however suffer greatly from a flare-up of my Bee Disease. There is no known cure to this horribly contagious illness, and sometimes it causes its victims to suffer terribly in a variety of ways.

When the bee supply catalogs began arriving in January, I looked through them, dog-earring the pages of items I wanted. OK, dog-earring every page. Seeing new honey containers and queen rearing equipment aggravated my Bee Disease. I wanted—no, I *needed*—to work my bees.

The weather is a major factor in my Bee Disease flare-ups.

At 8 degrees, I almost forget I have Bee Disease ... almost. I did steal outside to quickly take this picture.

When it is 8 degrees outdoors and snowing, I can almost forget that I have the disease. While my darling insect friends are clustered in their hives, I parallel their behavior and cluster on the couch with the cats.

At 18 degrees, the disease is generally quite tolerable. But when the mercury begins to climb over the freezing mark, I get a little itchy and restless.

Thus, on that unseasonably mild January day in Michigan when most of America suffered from the flu, I began to suffer from Bee Disease. I restlessly paced the house, looking out the windows to see if bees were flying.

When the mercury climbed to 48 degrees, I could stand it no longer and trotted to the apiary. A few bees had ventured out of each hive after months of being stuck inside in the dark. I greeted them. Silly, perhaps, but it seemed like the thing to do. Silliness and giddy behavior are also indicators of Bee Disease.

Occasional paralysis is another symptom. When the mercury hit 52 degrees, that happened to me. I had squatted near the entry of a hive, a front row seat from which to view bees staggering into the sunlight and taking long overdue cleansing flights. Spellbound by their joy, I was unable to move. Yes, this meant that I had yellow-brown spots[1] all over me. If you're a beekeeper, you're absolutely fine with that.

As I crouched by each hive, greeting each and every bee, the wind died down. Soon the pale winter sun shone steadily, and within minutes all the hives had erupted with activity. The bees looped and swooped (and pooped). Abuzz with shared excitement, I immediately called my husband at work.

"At work," I said. "All our hives are alive!"

He asked if the bees were as happy to see me as I was to see them. That was an interesting question. You see, I generally know what happy bees sound like and how they behave. But it was January, I'd sort of forgotten what happy bees look like. I remembered, with acute clarity, what unhappy bees look like. Even though the previous summer they'd flown at me at 200 mph with stingers in launch position, I remember quite clearly that those weren't happy faces.

Splitting a Hive

A strong colony propagates by separating into two or more colonies. Beekeepers often split their strong colonies into two colonies in the spring, in an attempt to prevent swarming and to increase the number of colonies.

I was buzzing the rest of that unseasonably warm day, dreaming about how with 14 hives alive in January, I could split them and have 28 hives in May. I tried to keep it all in perspective. Having bees alive in Michigan in January isn't that difficult. Having all those colonies still alive come April is the real challenge.

Michigan weather being, well, Michigan weather, within 24 hours those bees were back in a tight cluster as a winter storm barreled in. The driveway needed shoveling, there were icicles hanging from the roof as treacherous and dangerous as the roads. But, there were bees alive in my backyard, lots and lots of bees. When you have Bee Disease, that's all it takes to feel that all is right with the world.

---

1   Bees don't defecate in their hive unless they have illnesses, or can't get out after too many weeks inside. Thus, when there's a break in winter weather, bees will fly out to relieve themselves, and small yellow-brown spots will show up on area surfaces.

"Dad's" Bees

Our family has a large fruit and vegetable farm. Asparagus pokes up through the ground in spring, followed by blooming strawberries, cherries, apples, pears and peaches. Summer sees dozens of varieties of vegetables begging for pollination, and because of the bees' efforts, there are apples, squash and pumpkins in the fall. If any place needs bees, it's Corey Lake Orchards.

Back in the 60s and 70s, Mom managed two hives on the farm's 700+ acres. Undoubtedly they pollinated, but their main purpose was to keep four hungry kids in honey. We always had a sticky frame of honeycomb on the kitchen table, complete with telltale finger holes where we poked it for tastes.

Dad watching me work hives on the barn roof. That black dog? That's my loyal protector, Shiloh, sleeping of course.

Mom stopped keeping bees after most of us grew up and flew the nest. Farm activities had also grown, but more likely, she no longer felt the need to escape to the hives. Raising four spirited daughters was undoubtedly tough on Mom. Too often my sisters forgot that Mom liked me best. Sometimes even Mom forgot that.

Beyond Mom's few hives, there must have always been plenty of wild bees pollinating the farm. But, wild bees, like managed colonies, have been challenged by issues like the Varroa mite. Because the farm could use more pollinators, and because I'd already filled my suburban backyard with about all the hives my neighbors would tolerate, one winter Dad and I whiled away a few hours chatting about having managed bees on the farm again.

Dad was very wary of honeybees—probably years of working the fields make you guarded around stinging insects. But, he understood their key role, and appreciated them for the honey he'd drizzled on surely thousands of Mom's biscuits.

 © 2014 Charlotte Hubbard | www.hubbardhive.com

As the days began to lengthen, our weekly conversations about bees turned to where we'd put them. I reviewed the guidelines for the best placement of hives. Dad said he'd ponder possible locations.

Decades of farming took their toll on my Dad, both mentally and physically. Once he got to his eighties, there were many days when he didn't remember so well, and many other days when his gait was slow and unsteady. But through the increasing mental fog, somehow he remembered the guidelines for ideal locations. Each weekly visit he'd tell me about new spots he'd scouted. We finally decided on a low, flat barn roof near the house. It provided easy access for me, and easy observation for Dad and the customers who flock to the farm market.

The week my package bees arrived, Dad may have been even more excited than I was. He parked his lawn chair below the roof and watched the installation, although a few times he watched with his eyes closed. Perhaps he was strolling down memory lane, recalling when my late mother tended her hives. Or perhaps he just nodded off.

While Dad didn't initially know much about beekeeping, it turns out you *can* teach an old dog new tricks. Dad tagged along when I worked the bees, handing me the equipment after I got up on the roof, and helping light the smoker. By the end of the summer he had learned about brood patterns, drawn

What Are Those Terms?

Brood pattern refers to how the queen lays eggs in the honeycomb. If she deposits an egg in practically every cell in the majority of cells on the face of a frame of honeycomb, that's a great brood pattern.

Drawn foundation describes foundation after the honeybees have added wax to the human-provided starter sheets of wax or plastic. Honeybees secrete wax, and form those tiny bits to make perfectly shaped cells of the size they deem appropriate. (Drones need larger cells to grow in, so the worker bees form larger cells when drones are needed, for example.)

Drone-laying queens are queens who generally, mated improperly. They produce only male bees (or drones). The hive has no future without worker bees (those bees are sterile females). Worker bees tend the babies, forage for nectar and pollen, and keep the hive clean. A drone-laying queen, well, the most common way to deal with her is "off with her head!"

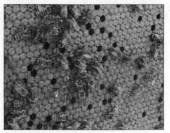

A great brood pattern!

foundation, and drone-laying queens. Unfortunately, he never learned how to keep our smoker going. That's probably because I was never able to teach him.

Our typical start-the-smoker session consumes about 50 matches, 10 yards of twine, a half bushel of dried leaves, pine needles, and wood shavings as well as at least half an hour.

Once, when lighting the smoker, Dad and I set a new record for re-lighting it. We were so exasperated that Dad finally suggested gasoline or a propane torch, noting we'd lit the smoker four times already and it just kept going out.

Four times? Ha. I had lost count after 10. Sometimes, a failing memory is a good thing.

That fall I was thrilled to be able to pull a few frames of the farm's first "managed" honey in decades. The market was thriving with folks seeking fall apples and cider. A few customers noticed the crazy person on the barn roof in a bee suit, and began watching. Dad was in his lawn chair in his usual back-of-barn location, also watching. I think he believed he could sprint over and catch me if I got too close to the edge of the roof, or maybe he just liked hiding behind the barn and catching a few winks.

Dad woke up to the crowd gathering around the back of the barn, from which they could better view me. He abandoned his chair (and my safety) and began telling the audience about "his bees."

Sharing honey and bees while Dad watches in his good pants.

 © 2014 Charlotte Hubbard | www.hubbardhive.com

"His bees?" I didn't recall him paying for the hives or the bees, or sweating atop the roof all summer, but maybe I was becoming forgetful also. The bees, whomever they belonged to, had definitely pollinated <u>his</u> crops. I decided to let his statement, well, bee.

The crowd grew to 18—grandfathers reminiscing about the good old days when practically everyone had a hive of bees, parents recalling tasting honeycomb as children, and kids peering cautiously at the giant man in stained bib overalls and his crazy daughter on the roof surrounded by stinging insects.

Atop the roof, I pulled a frame of honey and brushed off all the bees. I lay on my belly and handed it down to the outstretched hand of my father.

Dad grabbed it firmly with his thickly calloused, black-with-years-of-grease-and-grime fingers. Pulling out a pocket knife, he sliced into the golden cells and offered a taste of honey-dripping comb to anyone interested.

He had 18 takers.

The smiles on their faces confirmed that the bees had done well.

But no one's smile was broader than Dad's.

Beeks, Bearding and Other Oddities

There are many facets of beekeeping that are challenging to understand—starting with why anyone would do it. (Of course, when you're afflicted with Bee Disease, you don't understand why anyone would NOT do it.)

If you *unfortunately* don't yet suffer from the illness, here's a diagram offering one humorous explanation of beekeepers.

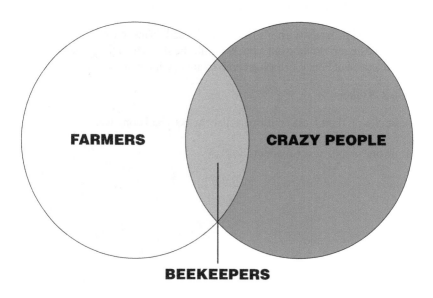

FARMERS   CRAZY PEOPLE

BEEKEEPERS

Like most things, beekeeping comes with its own, special vocabulary. Some of the terms are very suggestive of what they mean, like *hot hive*—a hive you want to handle like a hot potato. Bees *in* a hot hive are quickly coming *out* of it, bombarding you and sometimes stinging for no apparent reason. Working a hot hive will make you wonder why you keep bees.

Another unique term is *beek*. It's short for *beekeeper*, but is also a great combination word for people geeked about beekeeping.

One of my favorite not-so-obvious terms is *bearding*. Once you understand what it is, it's a great, descriptive word, and an even more awesome thing to witness.

Bearding typically occurs on a sultry late afternoon or evening, when the foragers return from the field. Worker bees at the hive are busy fanning to move air through the hive and dry the honey in an already overheated interior. Due to the high temperature, I suspect the foragers find it more appropriate to hang out on the "front porch" and discuss the events of the day, instead of adding to the heat of a fairly crowded hive.

Sometimes you'll find many of them fanning just outside the doorway, standing tiptoe on their back legs and moving their wings in a blur to pump air. Often times they're layered along the front of the hive and sort of kneading it—a behavior we can't yet explain.

Like a swarm, it is mesmerizing to see that many insects in one spot. And, like a swarm, they're fairly unconcerned about close-up observation. All of these photos were taken while wearing no protective clothing.

But yeah, that's a lot of bees isn't it? And way cool—says this total beek.

Two great examples of bees doing that bearding thing.

A Queen Bee to Be

Her brother was supposed to be the one.

Winter of '09, when friend Cris helped me sort through my late husband's bee equipment, I had shared my vast knowledge of beekeeping (then, a mere single season of stings and sweetness).

Cris, semi-fascinated with bees, felt her teenage son would be fully fascinated. When spring came, she wanted him to see how package bees were installed and what beekeeping was all about. Cris emphasized though that it would just be her son. Daughter Taylor was dreadfully scared of bees.

If you were to dissect a 14-year-old boy, I swear you'd find two 7-year-olds inside.

That spring, Cris brought her son to help install the bees, and 11-year-old Taylor tagged along. I was delighted by the opportunity to teach someone else about bees, but Taylor squished my enthusiasm by proclaiming she wanted NOTHING to do with them, she just came to videotape her brother. And that she'd be taping from inside, through the kitchen window.

I talked Taylor into at least putting on a bee suit and taping outdoors. It is tough to get good video through a window 50 feet from the apiary, especially my windows. I hadn't yet spring-cleaned them, for the fourth year in a row.

After taping the first installation, Taylor did creep a bit closer to the outside edge of the apiary. By the third installation, she'd slipped within spitting (or stinging?) distance. At the fifth installation she was the one who positioned the queen cage between two frames, and she practically installed the sixth package herself.

And her older brother, the one who we all thought would be interested in beekeeping? Well, he helpfully provided the muscle—carrying the bees from the garage to the apiary. But then, he asked if he could light the smoker, which he did easily (much to my shock), and then he strayed off to test it on a turtle. If you were to dissect a 14-year-old boy, I swear you'd find two 7-year-olds inside.

It was Taylor who helped me check the hives in a week, and helped me install

 © 2014 Charlotte Hubbard | www.hubbardhive.com

two more packages later that month. Her interest in bees seemed genuine, but I figured it was only a matter of months before her fascination with bees changed to a fascination with boys.

Surprisingly and wonderfully though, it continued. Like other fashionable preteens, Taylor sported crazy socks and funky earrings, but funky bee earrings. Unlike other fashionable preteens, she willingly wore an unfashionable bee suit to hang out in the apiary. She even took a few stings through those crazy socks.

It is a challenge to work bees with a non-beekeeper. They need to be able to take direction, and be attentive and calm in the face of tens of thousands of stinging insects in your face.

Able to take direction? Attentive? Calm? Not words typically used to describe an 11-year-old. Taylor, wonderfully though, was all of that. Unfortunately she was also a hive-tool-thin 11-year-old. Hard to lift a hive box when it weighs more than you.

Summer faded away, Taylor's interest did not. One chilly February, I joined her at her middle school's science fair night. People swarmed to our "All About Honeybees" classroom, with its free honey samples on graham crackers. At least they did until the Alligator/Other Reptiles Guy showed up and the crowd snaked over to his classroom.

Taylor was disappointed to lose her audience to harnessed baby alligators and snakes, but her (by then) 16-year-old brother, who was there to serve samples, was delighted to have all the graham crackers and honey to himself. If you were to dissect a 16-year-old boy you'd still get two 7-year-olds, accompanied by a 2-year-old.

Man-with-Boa-Around-His-Bicep's had his moment in the sun for a while, but then the crowds left there also, because the local hovercraft manufacturer made a late grand entrance in yes, a hovercraft. Next year, I'm thinking of taking live bees. While they don't make nearly as much noise as a hovercraft, when they fly down the halls they'll get a lot more attention.

The following summer, 13-year-old Taylor continued to "bee" with me. Her knowledge of the winged darlings has grown even faster than she has, along with her enthusiasm. How many other teenagers, drenched in sweat and stinging insects, will you find singing happily in a hot apiary? Even in the oven-like temperatures, working with her gives me goose bumps. Thank goodness there are kids like Taylor, the future of beekeeping.

Taylor and honeybees have a bee-utiful relationship.

But, deep inside that billowing beesuit, she is still a kid. When she leaves the apiary she immediately checks her phone and texts dozens of her dearest friends. I'm over 50, so of course, I don't get that texting thing as much.

Her messages though are things like "At work today I licked my fingers a lot," and "Keeping bees is the best thing ever!"

That part I get.

In Summary

Yes, I'm quite hopelessly addicted to honeybees.

Hopelessly and happily addicted. Thanks for buzzing along with me as I shared insights into the magical connection I've experienced with this insect.

For centuries, beekeeper-writers have tried to explain the intriguing link between our species. I think we've all fallen short. The only way to understand its glorious mystery is to experience it yourself.

If you do, undoubtedly you'll learn a great deal, and discover delight and laughter along the way. You may also experience a sting or two, but that's a small, temporary price to pay.

Pay it gladly, for beekeeping, like honey—well, nothing else compares to its pure sweetness.

Here's one of the joys of beekeeping—a frame of honey, bees calmly working it while I admire what they do.

For more about Charlotte Hubbard, her speaking events, publications, and humor-laced practical beekeeping advice, please visit *www.hubbardhive.com.*